M000201813

"An intriguing book about paren[...] [...]
porary societies around the globe[...]"

Alma Gottlieb, author of *The World of Babies*

"Synthesizes an impressive array of scientific data in an easy-to-read, even delightful, manner ... Particularly rewarding is its broad scope, weaving stories from scores of cultures across time and space, coupled with its intriguing focus. Readers who explore the universe of child-rearing techniques will gain insights not only into the human animal, but their own children as well."

Dr. Michael S. Sweeney, author of *Brain: The Complete Mind*

"A compelling compendium of cultural differences in childcare philosophy and child-rearing practices. He clearly demonstrates that the Western (middle-class) views and practices, which are offered in textbooks as the normal and healthy way, are at best an outlier in the worldwide spectrum. David Lancy says it is a book about parents, but it is also a book for parents, especially for Western middle-class parents, which would help them relax and rely more on their intuitions."

Heidi Keller, author of *Cultures of Infancy*

"David Lancy's tremendous first book, *The Anthropology of Childhood*, opened my eyes to child-rearing and parenting as products of culture, not nature. To me, a first-time parent, this gift of perspective helped me focus on what truly matters. Each essay in *Raising Children* packs the same punch. I'm giving this book to all the first-time parents I know."

Michael Erard, author of *Babel No More: The Search for the World's Most Extraordinary Language Learners*

"David Lancy's fascinating and comprehensive work on the anthropology of childhood puts modern Western parenting into much-needed historical and cultural context, calling into question all that we assume to be best practice or most 'natural.' In an age of unprecedentedly high parental anxiety, Lancy's work offers compelling, welcome evidence that there truly are many ways to raise a thriving child."

Christine Gross-Loh, author of *Parenting without Borders* and co-author of *The Path*

"If you've ever wondered why you are sitting on the toy-strewn floor, playing a third game of Candyland, so bored you are ready to hang yourself with a Slinky, Dr Lancy has the answer. It's the culture, not you."

Lenore Skenazy, founder of the book, blog and movement
Free-Range Kids

"Lancy is the rare academic who combines meticulous research and sharp storytelling skills with a big-hearted delight in the diversity of humankind. His work is erudite, wonderfully playful, and truly eye-opening for anyone who wants to know about the many valid approaches to parenting."

Mark Leviton, *The Sun* magazine (USA)

Raising Children
Surprising Insights from Other Cultures

Why, in some parts of the world, do parents rarely play with their babies and never with toddlers? Why, in some cultures, are children not fully recognized as individuals until they are older? How are routine habits of etiquette and hygiene taught—or not—to children in other societies? Drawing on a lifetime's experience as an anthropologist, David Lancy takes us on a journey across the globe to show how children are raised differently in different cultures. Intriguing, sometimes shocking, his discoveries demonstrate that our ideas about children are recent, untested, and often in stark contrast with those in other parts of the world. Lancy argues that we are, by historical standards, guilty of over-parenting, of micromanaging our children's lives. Challenging many of our accepted truths, his book will encourage parents to think differently about children, and, by doing so, to feel more relaxed about their own parenting skills.

David F. Lancy is Emeritus Professor of Anthropology at Utah State University. He is author/editor of several books on childhood and culture, including *Cross-cultural Studies in Cognition and Mathematics* (1983), *Studying Children and Schools* (2001), *Playing on the Mother-Ground: Cultural Routines for Children's Learning* (1996), *Anthropological Perspectives on Learning in Childhood* (2010), and *The Anthropology of Childhood: Cherubs, Chattel, Changelings* (2015).

Raising Children

Surprising Insights from Other Cultures

DAVID F. LANCY
Utah State University

CAMBRIDGE
UNIVERSITY PRESS

CAMBRIDGE
UNIVERSITY PRESS

University Printing House, Cambridge CB2 8BS, United Kingdom

One Liberty Plaza, 20th Floor, New York, NY 10006, USA

477 Williamstown Road, Port Melbourne, VIC 3207, Australia

4843/24, 2nd Floor, Ansari Road, Daryaganj, Delhi – 110002, India

79 Anson Road, #06–04/06, Singapore 079906

Cambridge University Press is part of the University of Cambridge.

It furthers the University's mission by disseminating knowledge in the pursuit of education, learning, and research at the highest international levels of excellence.

www.cambridge.org
Information on this title: www.cambridge.org/9781108415095
DOI: 10.1017/9781108227629

© David F. Lancy 2017

This publication is in copyright. Subject to statutory exception and to the provisions of relevant collective licensing agreements, no reproduction of any part may take place without the written permission of Cambridge University Press.

First published 2017

Printed in the United Kingdom by TJ International Ltd. Padstow Cornwall

A catalogue record for this publication is available from the British Library.

Library of Congress Cataloging-in-Publication Data
Names: Lancy, David F., author.
Title: Raising children : surprising insights from other cultures / David F. Lancy, Utah State University.
Description: Cambridge, United Kingdom ; New York, NY : Cambridge University Press, 2017. | Includes bibliographical references and index.
Identifiers: LCCN 2016059376| ISBN 9781108415095 (hardback : alk. paper) | ISBN 9781108400305 (pbk. : alk. paper)
Subjects: LCSH: Child rearing–Cross-cultural studies. | Parenting–Cross-cultural studies.
Classification: LCC HQ769 .L189 2017 | DDC 649/.1–dc23 LC record available at https://lccn.loc.gov/2016059376

ISBN 978-1-108-41509-5 Hardback
ISBN 978-1-108-40030-5 Paperback

Cambridge University Press has no responsibility for the persistence or accuracy of URLs for external or third-party internet websites referred to in this publication and does not guarantee that any content on such websites is, or will remain, accurate or appropriate.

Dedicated to my parents ... because they left me alone.

Contents

Figures

Acknowledgments

The idea that my obscure scholarship on the anthropology of childhood might serve as a lens through which to critically review contemporary child-rearing practices has been nurtured by many journalists and essayists. I cannot name them all but I can call out some of the most influential: Chris Shea of the *Boston Globe*; Michael Erard, well-known author of nonfiction; Lenore Skenazy, best-selling author of *Free Range Kids*; and Mark Leviton of *The Sun*. I thank Mike Sweeney, who tutored me on "trade" books, and Hara Estroff Merano, editor at *Psychology Today*, who invited me to become one of their bloggers. I am grateful, also, to Andrew Winnard of Cambridge University Press, who "sponsored" this volume as well as the second edition of *The Anthropology of Childhood*.

Katie Eyster has been a big help with research and improving my "outreach" through several dynamic websites. Last but not least, Jennifer Delliskave has been both a superb editor and a wonderful "informant" in the anthropological sense. As a very thoughtful mother of two, she has kept me from making assumptions about modern parenthood that were, in her view, off the mark. Friends (Hap Allen) and family (Joyce, Nadia) have fed me a steady stream of articles on modern parenting from the mass media.

1 Introduction

Leave the Kids Alone

It is a time-honored tradition in cultural anthropology that the researcher (referred to as an *ethnographer*) begins his/her narrative with a story or anecdote. This sets the scene, as it were.

The Maniq are one of the very last nomadic hunter-gatherer societies on earth. Maniq bands travel through and reside in the forests in the Khao Bantat mountain range of southern Thailand. They live in camps where each family builds a temporary hut from bamboo, banana leaves, and similar materials. Men hunt birds and mammals with poisoned darts propelled from a blow gun and also used spears in the past. They occasionally practice trapping and fishing and men climb trees to gather honey and fruit. Women and girls gather forest fruits, starches like taro and cassava, and tubers dug out of the ground with digging sticks. Maniq communities are small, tight-knit, and committed to an egalitarian and peaceful existence. Gathered foods and game acquired by hunters are widely shared—not just with immediate kin but with the entire band. Hunting weapons are never used for violence, public displays of anger are rare, and children are affectionately indulged by the entire community. This ethos is absorbed by children whose games have no winners or losers and play groups encompass virtually all the children in the community, regardless of age. Their make-believe play closely mimics the activities, particularly food gathering and preparation, of adults. They are welcome to participate in adult activity, including hunting and gathering, and they clearly learn from these experiences. While there is no coercion (the Maniq believe that trying to shape the child's behavior will make him/her ill) and no "curriculum," children effectively manage their own "education." Indeed, there are no words in their language for *teaching* or *learning*. Children become fully competent in the adult repertoire of skills

1

Figure 1.1. Maniq girl with knife

by fourteen, including the ability to independently navigate and exploit the forest's resources.

The Maniq move on when game in the area is thinned out. They travel lightly with very few "modern" materials. They have, however, acquired steel knives and machetes which get heavy use. The indulgence of children extends to permitting them, even crawling infants, to handle these sharp tools. A colleague of mine, Khaled Hakami, has carried out a long-term study of the Maniq and shared with me several of his on-site photos of children with knives. One photo shows a baby crawling along holding a fifteen-centimeter-long knife while her father looks on approvingly. A second photo (Figure 1.1) shows a girl of four wielding (e.g. cutting some vegetable material) a machete and a third shows a boy of, perhaps, six carefully using a fifteen-centimeter knife to prepare a rat he's caught for the stewpot. Hakami wrote in reply to my query, "They play and run with knives all the time. But I never saw a child get hurt when using a knife. On the contrary, at the age of four all children can easily skin and gut small animals." The Maniq are by no means unique in their laissez-faire attitude toward their children. Many, if not most, tribal societies expect children to take whatever risks are necessary to learn their culture, especially how to use tools and do useful things with them.

As remote—in every sense—as the Maniq seem to the audience for this book, I propose to draw at least two universal lessons about raising children from this example. First, all children seem to learn best when they can be "hands-on." Second, children who are not wrapped in cotton wool (e.g. overprotected) may develop several intangible virtues like resourcefulness, creativity, resiliency, and determination or "grit." I will expand on these two lessons in Chapter 5, but there are many other lessons we can learn by studying child-rearing practices in other cultures and in the past, a field of study to which I have devoted my career.

The immediate impetus for this book was a flattering article by Michael Erard in the *New York Times* about my recently published scholarly tome *The Anthropology of Childhood: Cherubs, Chattel, Changelings*. Titled "The Only Baby Book You'll Ever Need," the article had a salutary effect on sales and my editor at Cambridge University Press asked me if I'd consider writing a "baby" version of the book for a wider audience. And here it is! But before going further, I must provide a disclaimer. Contrary to the title of the *New York Times* article, neither the scholarly original nor this compact version of my work can in any way be construed as a substitute for Dr. Spock et al. It is a book *about* parents and children, not a *prescription* for how to do a better job of raising children. After all, I am, to the core, an academic—the leopard can't change its spots. With that warning, I'll allow that there is a very practical, down-to-earth message throughout this book: There's no such thing as a perfect child, and parents should absolve themselves of any sense of failure if their children don't quite reach perfection. Michael Erard clearly saw this as *the* main takeaway message from my book: "Children are raised in all sorts of ways, and they all turn out just fine."

Another reason this is not a childcare manual is that, as interesting and suggestive as traditional childcare notions are, the circumstances under which Western parents are raising their children are just too different from the cultural and historic examples I cite. Consider, for example, the notion that "it takes a village." This is a bedrock principle in the vast majority of the world's societies, both in the distant and the more recent past. It means that children are cared for by individuals, often several, in addition to the mother. Typically these include a grandmother and siblings. Their care permits the mother some respite; it permits her to do her "job," including taking care of a household, gathering, gardening, weaving, etc. It also permits her to recover her vitality and contemplate another baby. Having twins, or a toddler and an infant simultaneously, can be overwhelming, but much less so if one can expect "helpers at the nest." But we don't have a ready supply of helpers anymore. The precipitous decline in the birthrate that occurred during the last century has reduced the number of older siblings available as helpers. And grand-mothers, in our highly mobile society, are likely to live hundreds of miles from their grandchildren.

Sometimes those stark cultural differences can be informative, however. For instance, take the issue of privacy—especially for children. It is now considered the norm in well-off, postindustrial nations for children to have their own room. Often this room assignment occurs before birth in the creation of "the nursery." We can afford to allocate separate living areas to children, and with smaller families, children no longer need to share space with siblings. Comparatively speaking, the average American enjoys seventy-seven square meters of living space, residents of the UK thirty-three square meters and in Hong Kong fifteen square meters. But these are fully modern, wealthy societies. One can expect that in rural villages in the undeveloped world, there would be considerably less space per person. In Poomkara, a village in Southern India,

> Children could be everywhere in the house but could claim none of the spaces as theirs . . . Schoolbooks were often simply stuck under the palm roof and children's clothes hung on a rope. Children did their homework sitting on the same mat on which they slept at night. Even this mat was often shared with others.

This situation is absolutely commonplace. In fact, infants and young children are widely expected to sleep with their parents or other family members. A child that seeks privacy, or who prefers solitary to group play, will be considered abnormal—a cause for concern.

So, while we might feel that allocating personal space to children is a necessity—an entitlement—this is an extremely recent phenomenon and there's no evidence that children require private space. The children of Poomkara have none, expect none, and are not harmed when they get none. This contrast can be extended almost indefinitely. Village children eat what everyone else eats. There are no special children's foods (except for pablum and the like for toothless babies). Clothing is shared with others, as are playthings.

I think a discussion of contemporary norms regarding the granting of privacy to children can contribute much to a lessening of household conflict. Consider the long-term prognosis for the seemingly benign practice of "furnishing" the young child with not-to-be-shared resources. The child's room eventually becomes its kingdom, barred to anyone the child refuses to admit. That the room may be a filthy, untidy mess should be (from the child's perspective) no one else's business. Consider the distancing that can occur between children and their families once they acquire a smartphone. From age sixteen, the fortress-building fostered by the child's private bedroom expands with the adolescent acquiring his/her own vehicle. And so it goes, with frustrated parents referring to their pre-pubescent and adolescent offspring as "strangers" living under the same roof.

Space ownership is only one example from many we might discuss, but let's zoom out to the bigger picture. In my earliest attempt to review and synthesize the study of childhood by anthropologists, I constructed a simple model that helped me make sense of the most important "finding." I named this model "neontocracy" (us) versus "gerontocracy" (them).

This simple model crystalizes the contrast between "new" Western ideas about childhood and the ideas that have characterized humanity for millennia. Even prehistorical funerary remains bear out this juxtaposition of highly valued elderly and lowly children. That is, we can tell the relative worth of the deceased from the

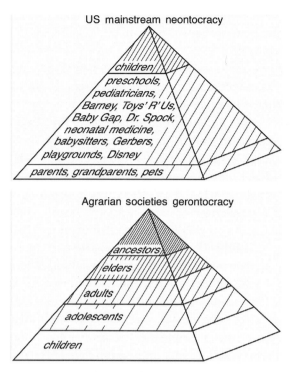

Figure 1.2. Neontocracy versus gerontocracy

location and richness of the interment, and these match the model. More recently, Joe Henrich and colleagues have developed a similar model based on a thorough analysis of the culture-bound nature of the discipline of psychology. They argue that research and theorizing about humans is based almost entirely on studies with samples from WEIRD (Western, educated, industrialized, rich, democratic) societies. They note that, where comparative data are available, people in WEIRD societies consistently look like outliers. Therefore, they argue, WEIRD subjects represent one of the worst subpopulations one could study for generalizing about *Homo sapiens*. Undoubtedly, granting a child a great deal of personal space is a practice found primarily in WEIRD society and reflects the values of a neontocracy.

As I have indicated, when I look at contemporary views on raising children from the perspective of many other societies, I see excessive concern for perfection. Perfect kids are raised by perfect parents, who draw their inspiration from best-selling child-rearing gurus who have all the answers. It wasn't always like this.

Historically and cross-culturally, child-rearing patterns were "customary," part of the suite of behaviors which every community member had ample opportunity to observe and emulate. Prospective mothers did not receive much in the way of "instruction." They were expected to have learned whatever was required from years of observation of mothering and from apprenticing as a caretaker of younger siblings. Further, the burden of child rearing and care was usually spread over a cadre of alloparents including grandmothers, aunts, and older siblings. This pattern is, inevitably, conservative. Significant innovation will be rare. Indeed, NGO and government interventions in rural, tribal communities to educate mothers in proper pediatric hygiene and medical treatment took many years before effecting change.

In the West, the transition from learning how to mother through observation and practice, to learning from doctors and their advice pamphlets, dates only from the 1830s. At that time, medical science began to have an impact on infant survival—primarily through the promotion of improved hygiene. Throughout the latter half of the nineteenth century, there was a growing gap between the survival and overall health of children whose mothers followed "tradition" and those who accepted the guidance of the medical profession. That this transition took so long was, in part, due to the fact that much of the medical advice was actually harmful. An example would be the advice to lance a baby's gums when teething begins.

Along with changes in child-rearing practice driven by the increasing authority of experts, there was the growing possibility of "failed" motherhood. That is, if experts took on the task of "scientifically validating" the advice contained in their manuals, it follows that mothers were liable to be blamed for the illness, death, or social and economic failure of their children. Society no longer looked to the child itself, the social and economic milieu it was raised in, or "God's will" as primary culprits in accounting for unfortunate outcomes. Failure had to be a lapse on the mother's part in faithfully enacting the programs designed by experts.

Current parental angst has its roots in this transition to using "expert" advice versus watching others and learning from their example. The reliance on "authorities," self-proclaimed or otherwise, has undermined any inherent confidence a prospective parent might feel about the task they're facing. Parental "instincts" are seen as untrustworthy. Contemporary parental advice rhetoric is loaded with terms like "natural," "normal," and "essential." These can be paired with "unnatural," "abnormal," and "neglectful." It is nearly impossible to objectively evaluate these admonitions and warnings, so one's selection from the menu of offerings depends mostly on how persuasive the expert is, and/or how similar the advice giver is to the advice seeker. Child-rearing practices are also inordinately shaped by movements (all organic, all the time), fashions (strollers for jogging), and panics (e.g. child abductions, vaccinations cause autism).

The archives of anthropology (reporting varied childcare strategies across cultures) and history (ditto across time) can provide us with a "crap detector" (with thanks to Hemingway). That is, we can compare what are currently considered "good" strategies for raising children with the patterns of the past. The goal is not to pit these ideas against each other to see who wins, but to tease out dramatic points of contrast, and to ask of the past, how were children raised? What views or ideas guided these practices and what were the outcomes? How does contemporary practice differ from more "traditional" (as recently as fifty years ago for readers who can recall) patterns? Can this backward or cross-cultural look shed light on contemporary issues? Read on; you'll be able to judge for yourself.

2 Culture and Infancy

Just over a decade ago, I began to work on a "Herculean task"—no one else had ever attempted to do it—the review, analysis, and synthesis of the literature in anthropology (later, history was added) on childhood. The lifespan covered ranged from the idea of having a child (who makes the decision, how is it made, what marriage has to do with it) to the adolescent's transition to adulthood. As a measure of the scope of this task, the reference list from the most recent edition of the book that ensued from this work, *The Anthropology of Childhood*, runs to over a hundred pages with nearly 2,000 distinct sources. The synthesis yielded one overarching conclusion: babies, or the children they might become, are thought of in entirely different ways across this wide sample of societies.

The subtitle of the book, "Cherubs, Chattel, Changelings," expresses my view that this variability can be captured in three prototypes. "Changelings" is a convenient label for the babies that are unwanted, unwelcome, or given only a conditional place in society. On Chuuk Island in Micronesia, for example, abortion "may be practiced if divination indicates that the child is a *soope* (ghost or spirit). If a child is born malformed ... it is sometimes killed for similar superstitious reasons." The survival or longevity of a changeling is in doubt.

"Chattel" describes the model where children are very welcome and the society embraces high fertility as an ideal. Women with many live children are valorized. But the babe's welcome is largely in anticipation of the work the child will—from a strikingly early age—contribute to the household. The Greeks used the same word, *pais*, to designate both child and slave. This anticipation is usually extended to the period when the parents are no longer self-sufficient. Ideally, many morally obligated children can be

9

expected to provide social security for elderly or disabled kin. Korowai "adults express an expectation of pleasurably consuming the bounty of a grown child's work." Viewing children as chattel is particularly true for agrarian peoples, farmers and herders.

"Cherubs" names a prototype where babies are welcomed for their own sake. As anthropologist Marjorie Shostak noted for the Kalahari Desert hunter-gatherers referred to as the !Kung, "children are valued . . . for their ability to make life more enjoyable." Before the postindustrial period, cherubs were few because the foraging way of life had become quite rare. Interestingly, as the !Kung inevitably adapted to a sedentary, subsistence-farming economy, their children transitioned from cherubs to chattel.

It follows that each of these archetypes engenders a different pattern of care. Changelings may be subject to neglect, compared to "normal" babies in the same society. Extreme neglect shading into infanticide is, or was, surprisingly common. The label and folk theory of "the changeling" may be used to justify the ill treatment.

Babies destined to be treated as chattel or cherubs can expect great attention and care to counteract the various threats to their viability. Strategies include: secluding the mother and infant for their health and safety; round-the-clock, on-demand nursing; long-term nursing to increase the intervals between births; the use of the services of a shaman and herbal medicines when the infant is ill; and swaddling them. Cherubs, but not chattel, are cuddled, kissed, sung to, spoken to, and played with; their genitals are stimulated, and they are never punished or scolded.

Of course, these distinctions may, at times, be blurry. Ache foragers in Eastern Paraguay almost never separate infants from their mothers, and babies may suckle whenever they choose; "they are never set down on the ground or left alone for more than a few seconds." However, anthropologists also report the case of an infant who was buried alive. They were told, "It is defective, it has no hair, besides, its father was killed by a jaguar." The Ache live on the thin edge of survival and children are readily sacrificed in response to such crises.

In the essays in this chapter, I expand on these themes, discussing the threats to an infant's well-being and strategies employed to reduce such threats. Interestingly, there is an inverse relationship between the prevalence of such threats (and effect on infant mortality) and the time, energy, and, above all, money spent on infant care. As our cherubs are more and more likely to survive, we continue to escalate our anxiety and intervention on their behalf. As the actual threats to infant well-being have dramatically declined, imagined and exaggerated threats, such as child abduction, have more than filled the vacuum.

Celebrating Babies

Every year at the beginning of January, our local newspaper runs a full-page, illustrated piece on the first New Year's baby born in the community. This article is only the most public celebration of the many related events which occurred throughout the previous year, as the parents eagerly anticipated the infant's arrival. They marked the baby's passage from idea to reality with a stream of vivid "Instagram moments." The creative pregnancy announcement, followed by semi-public den building as cribs and playpens arrived, and Disney-character wallpaper was plastered on the walls of the "nursery." Ultrasound pictures and videos of the fetus were shared on Facebook and passed around at family gatherings, accompanied by enthusiastic discussions of gender and naming (I've recently learned of the "gender reveal" party, which I at first thought meant "coming out of the closet" but then learned that it was an occasion to celebrate the first ultrasound image to indicate the fetus's sex). The "baby shower" widened the circle of celebrants, as will the naming and blessing ceremony following the birth.

Little do we appreciate how much we really have to celebrate. In earlier times and in many other societies, this unbridled optimism and public acclaim regarding the outcome of a woman's pregnancy would have been unthinkable. Here's a brief rundown of the perils that others have faced producing the next generation.

First, and most significantly, pregnancy itself often provoked an ambiguous reaction. While virtually all societies valued additions to the family—especially male—the probability that the mother would not survive the ordeal was so high that, for much of European history, for example, pregnancy was viewed as a disease. The mother's value to her family and community as a provider and caretaker of previous offspring is usually higher than the potential value of a new baby, hence her death or prolonged postpartum depression or disability might be a catastrophe.

Aside from worries about her health, a pregnant woman might be under a great deal of stress due to others carefully scrutinizing her behavior. Should she miscarry or give birth to a stillborn or deformed child, it will be assumed that the mother (or father) has violated either a specific taboo or a more general proscription, such as the commission of adultery or theft. She labors to observe a cornucopia of taboos regarding her diet, her clothing, where she travels, and whom she spends time with. Ironically, many of the food taboos and other proscriptions recorded were designed to "harden" the fetus, but may have actually diminished the mother's health and increased the risk of complications. Kaliai women from New Britain Island can't "eat wallaby because the child might develop epilepsy and have seizures during the full moon." Of course, foods are not the only things to be avoided. "In Fiji nothing tight must be worn around the mother's neck lest the umbilical cord strangle the fetus." For the same reason, Maisin (Sepik region of Papua New Guinea) mothers-to-be must not wear necklaces, make string bags, or encounter spiderwebs.

The expectant mother may become a target of suspicion (is the child legitimate?) or jealousy (from co-wives or barren women). In the Himalayan kingdom of Ladakh, women "hide or conceal their pregnancy to avoid the evil eye." In Gapun, another part of the Sepik region, "pregnancy [and childbirth] is considered to be an extremely vulnerable time . . . when sorcerers will not be able to resist the opportunity to kill [the mother] for some past wrong by shooting enchanted substances into her body to 'close' her so that the baby or the placenta will not be able to emerge." Once the

Gapun baby emerges from the womb, it will be secluded for months with its mother in a birthing house—a fairly common practice. For Tamils, the "childbirth house is completely shuttered and closed during the actual delivery and . . . much of the postnatal pollution period . . . in order to protect the mother and baby from marauding spirits, ghosts, and demons which are attracted to all the blood and contamination." Aside from these supernatural forces, seclusion may well shield the mother and baby from communicable illness.

In effect, the mother and child are quarantined for some period. This is not only designed to protect them from harmful forces, but also to protect others *from them*. The blood of childbirth and its liminal state are considered to be very dangerous and polluting. And, pragmatically, seclusion draws a discreet curtain, behind which the mother or her kin can elect to dispose of an unwanted infant. Among the Lepcha of Sikkim, the first three days of the newborn's life pass with no acknowledgment of its birth. In effect, it is still in the womb, and is referred to as "rat-child." Only after the house and its inhabitants have been thoroughly cleansed will the infant be welcomed into the world of humans with a special feast. This period of invisibility or nonpersonhood varies, depending on the rate of infant mortality. In ancient Greece, children under the age of two were never said to have died *ahoros*, "untimely." In societies with very high infant mortality, the child may not be acknowledged or named until it is eighteen months old.

The infant's vulnerability and helplessness may not provoke a strong nurturing response, but instead an emotional distancing or disdain. For example, "adults in colonial America viewed infants as rather inadequate creatures, extremely vulnerable to accident and disease, irrational and animalistic in their behavior." Similar views of infancy can be traced to the ancient Greeks. Anthropologist Christopher Little, writing about the Asabano of Papua New Guinea (PNG), explains that "infants are seen as non-sentient beings. When I would inquire about a baby, caregivers were quick to state that, s/he 'does not have thoughts' or that s/he 'is still breastfeeding' . . . similar language is used to describe dogs and bush animals."

By treating the infant as not fully human, the parents and community can more readily expose, abandon, or destroy it. Historically, most societies condoned infanticide for various reasons. For instance, forest foraging groups like the Tapirapé from central Brazil only allowed three children per family. Subsequent newborns had to be left behind in the jungle. This proscription was motivated by the ever-constant threat of starvation. Well past the neonate stage, infants were studied carefully for signs of physical or emotional abnormality. Should such signs emerge, it might be judged to be a changeling. "Sickly babies were impostors left by goblins in place of healthy ones." The infant left behind became an *enfant changé* in France, a *Wechselbag* in Germany, in England a "fairy child." In northern Europe, changelings were left overnight in the forest. If the fairies refused to take it back, the changeling would die during the night—but since it was not human, no infanticide could have occurred. Among the Dogon of Mali, children thought to be evil spirits were taken "out into the bush [where] . . . they turn into snakes and slither away . . . You go back the next day, and they aren't there. Then you know for sure that they weren't really children at all, but evil spirits."

Dramatic and welcome changes have occurred over the last fifty years, particularly in the industrialized nations, so that we may bring our babies out of the shadows and celebrate their arrival. The death of the mother in childbirth is now extremely rare and infant mortality has fallen precipitously. Child mortality has fallen as well. We can attribute these gains to improved nutrition and prenatal care, and more hygienic birthing practices. Indeed, the "advice-to-mothers" manuals from the nineteenth century focused on the challenge of keeping the infant alive. The decline in the birth rate, and safe, affordable contraception, have also contributed to improved maternal health and reduced infant mortality rates. Unlike their sisters in many less developed areas, women in wealthier nations can elect to become pregnant and bear a child when they are physically, emotionally, and financially "ready." The majority of our children are now born with joyous anticipation.

Meanwhile, however, as we celebrate our babies, we must guard against complacency. In many Third World countries, conditions for infants and their mothers have changed little from those described above. And, in the USA, the record, when it comes to mother–infant health, is abysmal. The infant mortality rate is higher than sixty other nations. Compared to other developed countries, US rates of premature birth, fetal exposure to drugs (including alcohol and nicotine), child abuse, and murder are very high. These unfavorable outcomes are driven by the high birth rate overall, and especially the rate of unwanted births among women living in poverty. In fact, each additional birth leaves a mother worse off economically. International child welfare surveys are regularly carried out by the OECD, the CIA, and UNICEF. These surveys show that the USA rate of teen pregnancy—with predictably bleak outcomes for the child—is among the highest in the world: four times the European Union average. Advances in genetic counseling, child nutrition, inter-birth spacing (IBI), contraception, and sex education are unavailable or ignored by many prospective parents, condemned by many religious groups, and rejected by politicians. Access to family planning services is becoming more restricted in the US as the need—in terms of the growing population of mothers living in poverty—is increasing. While there is much to celebrate in terms of child and infant welfare, many women and their infants still face a bleak prognosis.

What about Swaddling?

Pioneering anthropologist Margaret Mead wrote what may be seen as the epitaph for swaddling babies in 1954. She noted, "the idea of swaddling is peculiarly horrifying to Americans, one of whose major commitments is to freedom of movement." But I sense a gradual rehabilitation under way. This is being driven in part by the same forces that promote breast-feeding and organic baby foods—it seems "natural." Also, empirical evaluation of the practice does show measurable benefits—in sleep quality, for example. Sleep quality is associated, in turn, with later health issues, such as obesity. One study "showed that, when infants between 6 and 16 weeks of age sleep swaddled and supine, they sleep longer, spend more time in NREM sleep, and awake less spontaneously than when not swaddled." On the other hand, there are a few sources that warn against swaddling, citing concerns about hip deformity, inadequate weight gain, hyperthermia, and SIDS—none of which have been empirically demonstrated.

Viewing swaddling as "natural" arises primarily from the ubiquity of the practice. It was practiced across all classes of society. Historian Karin Calvert writes,

> swaddling immobilized the child. Parents could hang the bound infant up on a nail and go about their business, secure in the knowledge that he couldn't crawl into the fireplace or fall down a well. A swaddled baby, like a little turtle in its shell, could be looked after by another, only slightly older, child without too much fear of injury, since the practice of swaddling made . . . child care virtually idiot-proof.

Anthropologists describe swaddling in cultures around the world. Nomadic herders, like the Pashtu, extoll the virtues of swaddling (full-time, night and day) and explain that

> the baby's flesh is *oma* (unripe) like uncooked meat, and that only by swaddling will it become strong (*chakahosi*) and solid like cooked (*pokh*) meat . . . a baby [may] whimper . . . or cry when . . . unwrapped from its "cocoon" for feeding and/or cleaning purposes [but] immediately quiets again when [re]wrapped and tied up.

Swaddling is also seen as efficacious in protecting the baby from harmful influences, such as the evil eye.

One of the most interesting forms of swaddling is the *manta* pouch used by Quechua farmers who live high in the Andes. It turns out this low-tech device is quite effective in promoting the infant's well-being in a harsh climate.

> Raising the temperature and humidity reduces the energy
> demands on the infant to warm and inspire air and . . . the manta
> pouch . . . increases the likelihood that the infant will sleep . . .
> mothers kept the infants in the pouch when nursing . . . little
> interaction took place . . . This pattern reduces the likelihood of
> arousing the infant. Each of these features may save only a little
> energy, but, in sum, a significant number of calories may
> be saved.

However, even in tropical countries where swaddling might lead to overheating, babies are preferably confined by a light cloth tied to the mother's back or hip (depicted in Egyptian tomb reliefs from 2500 BCE). In the New Guinea Highlands, the baby is placed in a mesh sack (*bilum*) "which hangs constantly from the mother's head, providing the external equivalent of the *man am* [womb, literally child house] . . . and can if necessary be suckled in route while the mother's hands remain free for foraging."

Swaddling and/or attaching the baby via a cloth or mesh fabric to its mother is supplemented, in many societies, by the use of other confining devices such as a cradleboard. Undoubtedly the Navajo were among the best-known exponents of the cradleboard, and some Navajo mothers continue using it today. There were four graduated sizes, designed to be lashed to a horse's saddle in such a way that a kind of awning could be stretched from the saddle bow over the cradle to shield the child. Of course, the board kept the child tranquil and out of its mother's way, but the Navajo had an elaborate rationale for its use, e.g. "Babies are kept . . . in the cradle to make them straight and strong. Some women let their children lie on sheepskins and roll about, but they are always weak, sick children."

Traveling in Uzbekistan in 2007, I discovered that a "modernized" version of the cradleboard is very popular and sold in every market. The child is swaddled and strapped into the cradle, which is sometimes fitted with rockers so the baby can, in effect, rock itself to sleep. Like a miniature four-poster bed, the cradle can be covered to block out the light. Most ingenious is a funnel arrangement that drains the infant's urine into a collector under the cradle.

In the USA and Europe, receptivity to swaddling and similar constraints is mediated by prevailing views on the nature of infancy. Americans are famously individualistic and ascribe unique personality, needs, and preferences to infants. Therefore they may be less likely to impose restraints, including "schedules," on their children than their European and East Asian counterparts. US parents talk to and otherwise stimulate infants, who are kept in a state of "active alertness," displaying early signs of intelligence and cognitive ability. The Dutch, by contrast, believe that all infants develop best via a regulated regime that emphasizes consistent and durable sleep patterns and, otherwise, a state of quiet alertness. Not surprisingly, US parents expect their babies to be "difficult," especially when it comes to nighttime rest. The concerns about swaddling—noted in my introduction—can be met with common sense: don't wrap the blanket too tight, and use a lighter-weight blanket because the baby will be encased in multiple layers. To learn more about contemporary swaddling practices in the USA, *The Happiest Baby on the Block* is one source.

There Was an Old Woman ...

> There was an old woman who lived in a shoe.
> She had so many children, she didn't know what to do.
> She gave them some broth without any bread;
> She whipp'd all their bums, and sent them to bed.

Like most nursery rhymes, "The Old Woman and the Shoe" expresses a universal truth. Jonathan Swift wrote in 1729,

> It is a melancholy object to ... see the streets ... crowded with beggars of the female sex, followed by three, four, or six children, all in rags, and importuning every passenger for alms ... instead of being able to work for their honest livelihood, [they] are forced ... to beg sustenance for their helpless infants who, as they grow up, turn thieves for want of work.

He proposed as a (satirical) solution to the problem of surplus children, the following: "a young healthy child well nursed, is, at a year old, a most delicious, nourishing and wholesome food, whether stewed, roasted, baked, or boiled; and I make no doubt that it will equally serve in a fricassee, or a ragout."

This message regarding the negative consequences for children of unchecked fertility still applies today. For example, the popular press carried a story (not satire) about an Albanian mother who'd given her three-year-old to an older, childless Italian couple in exchange for a television set and the promise of future payments. When these were not forthcoming, she complained to the authorities. In spite of living in such severe poverty that she was forced to sell her children, the woman had recently given birth to her eighth child. While the Albanian "old woman in a shoe" may be unusual, anthropologists have described numerous societies where high fertility, regardless of the consequences, is positively sanctioned.

In a famous study, Nancy Scheper-Hughes documented the phenomenon of infant neglect leading to death that is widely accepted as normal. The very poor women of Ladeiras, northeast Brazil, are "used up" (*acabado*) from too many previous pregnancies, and transfer this weakness to the fetus, which is then born frail and skinny, unfit for the *luta* (fight) ahead. A mother is, therefore, not held accountable for the infant's death. The cultural basis of reproduction in this community is completely Darwinian—of the many offspring, only the fittest will survive. Other scholars have documented similar conditions of extreme poverty associated with a fatalistic attitude to childbearing.

High fertility is valorized, regardless of circumstances. A prolific Fulani (Burkina Faso) mother is esteemed while her less prolific counterpart is scorned. "One man in his sixties, who had been through several wives, said, 'you cannot love your wife if she gives you no children.'" In spite of the high rate of infant sickness, malnutrition and death,

There are no perceived disadvantages in having lots of children. Children are never seen as a drain on resources. The availability of food is believed to be purely a product of the God-given fortune of the child, and nothing to do with the level of resources available within the household or the number of mouths to feed: "*BiDDo fuu rimdatakena e tindem*—every child is born with its own luck."

This cavalier attitude toward the child's well-being is by no means universal. Many, perhaps the majority, of the world's societies follow customs designed to improve the child's prospects. The practice of frequent, round-the-clock nursing releases prolactin, which in turn reduces the likelihood of pregnancy. Prolonged (three years +) nursing yields longer inter-birth intervals, as does the postpartum sex taboo. In Papua New Guinea, for example, the Enga see the man's semen as a component of his war magic. If this potent substance were to mix with breast milk, the result for the infant could be fatal. These customary practices enhance both the mother's and the infant's health. Among the Airo-Pai foragers of Amazonian Peru,

> Men and women have explicit ideas about family size and spacing. They say that the ideal number of children is three and that a woman should not become pregnant until her last child is capable of eating and moving around independently . . . Long birth spacings are necessary to provide an adequate upbringing for young children . . . closely spaced children are said to suffer, cry and develop angry characters.

Another widely employed practice is fosterage, in which families with too many children transfer their surplus to kin who have too few children.

Until the nineteenth century, Western Europe had a dismal record on the subject of fertility and child welfare. Not only was there no effective contraception, but any attempt to limit fertility was condemned as sinful. Infant and child mortality was so high in the Middle Ages that those who died were rarely given formal burials. They were, rather, buried as waste. Analyzing these pathetic remains, "archeology corroborates the impression given by the texts. Skeletons [of children exhibit] deep lesions, wounds, decalcification, bad teeth, in short, a state of relatively poor health." During this period, the sale of surplus children was widespread, e.g. "peasants of southern Italy got rid of their children at the marketplace during a large fair."

The Christian church offered a mixed blessing. In simultaneously banning infanticide *and* contraception, it forced mothers to abandon their surplus children. The response to this very public display of sick and malnourished children was to bundle them into foundling homes. Called *brephotrophia*, the earliest opened in Milan by the end of the eighth century CE. The supply of orphanage beds and food could never keep up with demand. The Ospedale degli Innocenti in Florence (one of sixteen *brephotrophia* in Tuscany alone) admitted 100 infants in its first year, admitting as many as 1,000 babies per year in succeeding years, two-thirds of whom perished before their first birthday. It was widely acknowledged that "being sent to foundling homes presaged early death." Children that survived infancy were treated little better than slaves, and in the early colonial era, thousands were involuntarily shipped to the colonies as agricultural laborers. Meanwhile, the well-to-do also had reason to limit fertility but lacked a legal and socially acceptable means to do so. Hence they winnowed their offspring via "maltreatment," as records showing *higher* infant and child mortality among the gentry than among peasants suggest.

The Industrial Revolution had a major impact on child-rearing cost–benefit calculations as factories offered parents the opportunity to earn wages through their children. While the size of one's landholding limited the scope for child employment, the Industrial Revolution encouraged a rise in fertility levels. By the 1720s, four-year-olds were employed in French textile mills, and 100 years later, in Lancashire, one-quarter of all ten- to fifteen-year-old girls were making cotton in factories. Restrictions were gradually imposed so that, by 1830, factory workers had to be at least eight years old, yet a working day of over fourteen hours was the norm, and they could be beaten for tardiness. However, outside the rural farm and urban proletariat, high fertility grad-ually began to lose its cachet.

The Quakers, at the end of the eighteenth century, became the first polity to deliberately limit fertility—in sharp contrast to the Puritans 150 years earlier.

> Relying primarily upon abstinence, *coitus interruptus*, and the rhythm method, supplemented by abortion (usually chemically induced or a result of trauma to the uterus), parents dramatically reduced [fertility] . . . The drop in the birthrate also reflected new cultural ideals, including a rejection of the view that women were chattel who should devote their adult lives to an endless cycle of pregnancy and childbirth.

Fertility decreased significantly during the second half of the twentieth century following what has been called the "great" or demographic transition. Many factors were involved, including the reduction of opportunities to earn an economic return from one's children; the transition to nuclear families and loss of extended-family members as child minders; and the need for more education, thereby delaying marriage and family formation. Urbanization provided better employment prospects for those who made a bare living caring for children. There was also the growing appreciation of how expensive it is to support children through the years of schooling required for steady employment and the maintenance or improvement of one's class standing. And, perhaps most important, children gradually acquired emo-tional and social value for parents rather than being seen, primar-ily, as "helpers" in the present and caretakers in the future. Quality now trumps quantity.

As laudable as these changes have been, several desirable attri-butes of premodern infancy have been lost. Chief among these is the loss of "mother's helpers." High fertility was sustained by the availability of a "village" of caretakers who could relieve the mother of significant portions of the burden of childcare. In many tribal societies, there is the belief that infants suffer if they do not have opportunities to interact with and form attachments to a variety of kinsmen, especially older siblings and grandmothers. These infants learn early how to discern and deal with varied personalities and the effects of gender and age on people's reaction to children.

As more of the world's peoples have gained access to family planning services, as well as pre- and postnatal care, fertility is declining overall. Nevertheless, there remain pockets of poverty and relative affluence where high fertility is still preferred and practiced. Even when tribal women are aware and desirous of using modern contraceptives, access may be denied them—with tragic consequences.

In some communities, such as the Shipibo Indian village of Manco Capac in the Peruvian Amazon, people are desperate for contraceptives—which they've heard about but cannot obtain. Anthropologist Warren Hern describes the plight of these Indians as dire:

> Chomoshico was nearing the end of her eleventh pregnancy. She already had seven living children. Neither she nor her husband wants more. "Enough. Clothes cost," they told me. "I'm tired of having children," she said. "I almost died with the last one." Her husband has tuberculosis. In the same village, a few weeks before, a young girl died on her thirteenth birthday trying to give birth to twins. And in that girl's natal village, up the river, I had just seen my first case of frank starvation among the Shipibo Indians, with whom I had worked . . . since 1964.

Scientists can now compare otherwise similar communities who share the same access to resources, but where large versus small families are preferred. The quantity-versus-quality trade-off has been measured empirically. In US studies spanning thirty-five years, children born into large families have lower expectations for academic success and life chances. In one study, for example, the authors conclude, "mothers and fathers can only achieve large family size at a significant cost to the quality of care provided to individual children. In fact, family size was the strongest explanatory variable considered in our analysis." In spite of these indicators, women encounter barriers in their attempts to limit their fertility—from religious sanctions, to machismo husbands, to patriarchal government attitudes. Around the world, fundamentalist religious tenets encourage childbearing. For example, in my home state of Utah and the surrounding border areas dominated by adherents of the Mormon faith, large families are the norm. This pro-natalist culture has come to national attention in the last decade with several television series highlighting fundamentalist Mormon (FLDS) polygamy and the prosecution of FLDS elders for impregnating their child brides.

Some subcultures that support high fertility tend to foster teenage pregnancy or the early onset of reproduction and short inter-birth intervals. Both of these trends are in turn predictive of premature delivery, low birthweight, and other adverse outcomes. These practices lead to lower-quality infants with impaired mental functioning and chronic illness. And the costs do not fall only on the child and its family. The very costly, taxpayer-funded services provided by the rapidly growing field of neonatal medicine are driving up medical costs overall.

Given these trends, it should be self-evident that cutting off government support for family planning services—a very popular idea in the US—will have deleterious effects on women and their offspring, as well as add significantly to the costs of state-provided welfare, mother and child health care, and police services.

3   Questions about Infant Attachment

The debates regarding parenting practices have become so polemical that the term "Mommy Wars" has entered the common vocabulary. Actually, the reach of the debate is broader and we should begin talking about "Parenting Wars." One of the latest battlefields is "attachment parenting," which focuses attention on the bonding between an infant and its mother (and father, too). Few "buzzwords" that have captured the attention of parents and childcare experts can match "attachment" for impact and controversy.

In the middle of the last century, John Bowlby, an English psychoanalyst, advanced a set of ideas about the emotional ties between a mother and her child now widely known as "attachment theory." Bowlby was interested in overturning the Freudian notion that the Oedipal complex made close relationships between mothers and sons very risky and unnatural. The theory has since then gathered adherents across a broad spectrum—from experimental psychologists testing for evidence of "secure" versus "avoidant" or "ambivalent/resistant" attachment, to social workers who point to "reactive attachment disorder" as the root of criminal behavior. More recently, attachment theory has morphed into a kind of secular religion where mothers worship at the altar of "attachment parenting."

This movement is well represented in two Web-based organizations. Attachment Parenting International promotes a variety of strategies to tighten bonds between children and mothers, including lengthy prescriptions for "baby wearing," and how best to play with one's child. The goal of Attachment.org is to provide help for "each wounded child with attachment disorder, [which is caused by, for example] 'caring for baby on a timed schedule or other *self-centered* parenting.'" As one indication of how far this movement

25

has progressed, parents are now urged and trained to "attachment-parent." So a rather abstruse and unsubstantiated theory has gradually evolved into a suite of childcare obligations as sacred as vaccination.

One confirmed apostate of the new attachment-parenting faith is noted media personality Erica Jong. She characterizes attachment parenting as: "You wear your baby, sleep with her and attune yourself totally to her needs [then wonder how you can] do this and also earn the money to keep her." Another critic has written an article, "The Perils of Attachment Parenting," which argues that attachment parenting puts the child's needs above the parent's, to the detriment of both.

Attachment parenting is one of the few parenting movements that draws explicitly on our studies of tribal societies for inspiration and justification, leading to statements like, "There's nothing new about Attachment Parenting; parents have been doing it naturally for as long as humans have existed." And, if the cornerstone obligations of attachment parenting are limited to "co-sleeping," "on-demand feeding," and keeping the child in constant contact with the mother, then it is assuredly true that these practices are characteristic of child rearing in most of the world's 1,000-plus distinct societies.

Yet anthropologists and comparative psychologists increasingly disavow the underlying tenets of attachment theory, as evidenced in two recent collections of scholarly papers. In the essays in this chapter, I will review the rich literature on the role culture and environment play in infant care. In the process, I hope to clear up this apparent paradox. In brief, I believe the paradox arises because the same practices (co-sleeping, for example) mean something quite different in modern bourgeois society than they do in the various small-scale traditional societies where it is commonly practiced.

Anthropologists studying mother–infant relations provide ethnographic descriptions that don't square with the attachment parenting orthodoxy. Anthropologist Gerald Erchak, working in rural Liberia, describes casual nurturance, where Kpelle mothers "carry their babies on their backs and nurse them frequently but do so without really paying much direct attention to them; they continue working or ... socializing." Paradise records, "When a [Mazahua] mother holds a nursing baby in her arms she frequently has a distracted air and pays almost no attention to the baby." LeVine observed "Gusii mothers [who] rarely looked at or spoke to their infants and toddlers, even when they were holding and breast-feeding them." In none of these cases did the anthropologists observe any decrement in the mental health of individuals sub-jected to—in attachment orthodoxy—maternal deprivation.

Returning to the paradox introduced earlier, we will see that all the so-called "natural" infant care practices are designed for the well-being and convenience of the mother, and only secondarily the infant. For instance, nursing 24/7 accomplishes two things. First, it keeps the infant in a quiescent state so they won't fuss, fully awaken, and require more attention. Second, nursing 24/7 promotes the production (in the mother) of prolactin, a hormone that acts like a contraceptive, reducing the new mother's chances of getting pregnant too soon or until her vitality has been restored and her infant is old enough to be weaned. Co-sleeping permits nursing at night without fully waking either mother or infant. And keeping the baby in close proximity—carried by an older sibling as a "helper at the nest" or attached to the mother's body by some device—may or may not strengthen emotional bonds, but, like the other practices, it allows the mother to nurse without interrupting whatever she's doing (working, gossiping, sleeping).

Even if we limit our comparative analyses to modern Western societies, there's hardly unanimity when it comes to attachment parenting. "British psychologist John Bowlby had a very limited influence [in Sweden], unlike in the UK and the USA. Swedish psychologists and psychiatrists resisted his emphasis on the attachment between mother and children, arguing for more modern, institutional solutions to family problems."

In a study with Karin Norman on mainstream German infant care practices, Bob LeVine demonstrated that the cases above are hardly exotic cultural outliers. Like Asian and French approaches, but unlike mainstream American practices, the German child-rearing model does not place the child at the center of the family. Its needs are met while maintaining normal, pre-birth family routines. Further, the German model safeguards against the child becoming "spoiled," *verwöhnt*, by excessive attention and too much accommodation to its needs and demands. Consequently, two-thirds of a middle-class German sample, following assessment with the "Strange Situation" protocol used to test the "security of attachment," were classified as "insecurely attached." As there is not a shred of evidence for widespread personality disorder in the area where the study was undertaken (Bielefeld), the authors argue that Bowlby's theory, while appropriate for discussing institutionalized and criminally abused or neglected children, has no currency in the context of most families.

Detachment Parenting

Based on the results of a thorough survey of the ethnographic, archaeological, and historic records on the subject of infancy, I propose to offer an alternative view of culture, biology, and the emotional experience of infants. After careful analysis of over 200 cases, the evidence suggests that, for the majority of societies, insufficient attachment is not a problem. On the contrary, I found elaborate models of infancy and childhood that seem to have been *constructed expressly to discourage exclusive emotional ties* to the newborn. Outside contemporary middle- and upper-class society, a number of unfavorable issues face the mother of a newborn, which has led to a broad consensus that the infant is not fully human. I will briefly review each of these factors in turn. Not all are equally potent in every society.

High Infant Mortality and Chronic Illness

We have good infant mortality data from a range of societies— from prehistoric settlements, nomadic foragers, and farmers, to complex societies in Europe and Asia. These data suggest that one-fifth to one-half of babies didn't make it to their fifth year. We can extrapolate from these figures to conclude that miscarriages and stillbirths were also common by comparison with current levels. Likewise, we can expect that if half the children died, then somewhat more than half were seriously ill in childhood. Indeed, in many villages in the global South studied by anthropologists, the level of clinical malnutrition was (and still is in many cases) 100 percent, as was the level of chronic parasite infestation and diarrhea. These unfavorable odds create a climate that supports withholding emotional investment in the newborn and maintaining a degree of emotional distance. This bleak picture characterized Western society as well. Childhood, according to the seventeenth-century French cleric Pierre de Bérulle, "is the vilest and most abject state of human nature, after that of death."

The Mother's Vulnerability

Another inexorable factor affecting the newborn was the threat it represented to its mother. Throughout much of human history, pregnancy was treated as if it were a serious illness. "A pregnant woman has one foot in the grave," according to a proverb from Gascony. Childbirth was, until recently, extremely risky. Even if the mother survived, she might become the target of jealousy and witchcraft on the part of human and non-human adversaries. She and the babe were both contaminated by the process of birth and the spilling of puerperal blood. Women were also made vulnerable by the need to obey food taboos at critical junctures such as menstruation and pregnancy. These taboos often involved restricting their intake of high-quality fat- and protein-rich foods. But most critical is the fact that the new mother was/is also likely responsible for maintaining a household; caring for husband, older children, and parents or parents-in-law; and making a major contribution to subsistence or the domestic economy through, for example, craftwork. The health and recovery of the mother was seen as far more urgent than the emotional health of the infant:

The [new Ladakh] mother is plied with foods [to] regain her strength. Her health is paramount—to care for the baby and to get back to the routine household and agricultural tasks upon which the success of the household depends—while household members simply hope for the best with regard to the newborn.

Alloparenting and Fostering

At the peak of her childbearing years the young mother is also a critical contributor to the household economy. Hence most societies embrace "alloparenting" as the means to lighten the mother's burden and thereby increase her fertility and her productivity. Numerous studies underscore that infants are tended as often by an alloparent—a grandmother, aunt, or older sibling—as by the mother. Further, the widespread prevalence of wet-nursing, adoption, and fostering, and, less commonly, the sale of infants, suggests that the bond between mother and child should be, preferentially, "weak":

> While awake, [Nigerian] Hausa infants are almost always in close physical proximity to one or more adult caregivers . . . infant signals, such as crying, are responded to promptly by adults or older children . . . Although Hausa infants appear to be attached to three or four different figures (including fathers), most are primarily attached to one. Importantly, the principal figure is not necessarily the mother, who is solely responsible for feeding, but rather the person who holds and otherwise interacts with the infant the most.

In contrast to shared motherhood as women make vital contributors to the household economy (they are "working moms"), the idea of a "stay-at-home" mom is a historical anomaly. Well-to-do women, throughout history, have stayed at home/not gone out to work largely as a mark of their husband's wealth and standing. And, while they might engage in some work at home as a demonstration of virtue (Greek women made textiles), their offspring were cared for by wet nurses, nannies and the like. Only since the mid-nineteenth century has the middle class reached a level of prosperity sufficient to relieve a woman of the need to work outside the home or to do paid craftwork in their home. This "norm" was suspended during both world wars and during the Great Depression, and seems to be rapidly disappearing among contemporary middle-class families.

Dysfunctional Families

The flip side of alloparenting—the "it-takes-a-village" childcare pattern—is that, in some societies, strife within the extended family is endemic, leading to chronically dysfunctional families. Indeed, conflict is so much a part of daily life that it is reflected in the folk model of infancy. Mothers are enjoined to roll their infants in dung, refer to them with bad names, and disguise their sex (if a boy), all in an effort to deflect the envious thoughts and machinations of other women in the household and neighborhood. There may also be tension between the mother and her husband if there's some doubt about paternity. Either parent might be seen as having a tendency to stray from fidelity. The newborn is often a lightning rod for these electric currents, and may be kept discretely sequestered for quite some time.

> Sorcery is considered to be the most important reason for a [Burkina Faso Papel] child's death. It is seen as a serious . . . problem. Because of envy, hatred, vindictiveness, or simply bad intentions some people decide to use sorcery to hurt a rival or someone they dislike. A child is often the chosen victim.

Infant Unwanted or on Probation, Leading to Neglect, Abandonment, and Infanticide

Only a tiny fraction of the world's societies accords an unconditional welcome to every new member. In societies where well-formed, full-term newborns may not survive to become helpful and able to pay back the investment made in them, the actuarial odds dictate a very careful evaluation of the newborn. Is it completely whole? Does it behave normally, crying neither too little nor too much, for example? Is it a girl when a boy is preferred? Did it arrive "too soon" before its older, and hence more valuable, sibling had been weaned? Is it unquestionably the offspring of its mother's husband? Does the mother have a husband? There are many negative attributes of the infant that would preclude attachment, including the following.

- "Illegitimate [Amazonian Mundurucu] children are usually killed at birth, along with twins and children with birth defects. If the child does survive it is referred to as '*tun*' which means excrement. They are not abused, but they cannot marry due to their indefinite status."
- "Among the Songye [of Ghana], those defined as 'bad' or 'faulty' children, including albino, dwarf, and hydrocephalic children, are considered supernaturals who have been in contact with sorcerers in the anti-world; they are not believed to be human beings, and they are expected to die."
- "Exposure was widespread in the ancient world, where reliable means of preventing conception were not widely used and abortion was dangerous for the mother ... parents would feel they could not make the investment of time, resources and emotion in raising a severely disabled child ... moreover ... there was the belief that such 'monsters' were sinister prodigies that needed to be expiated by the infant's death."

Utilitarian View of Offspring

The society that spawned and embraces attachment parenting is comparatively wealthy, well educated, and enjoys low infant and maternal mortality and a low birth rate. Children no longer provide material rewards to the parents who raised them, but rather emotional rewards and satisfaction. Elsewhere, each newborn is/was subjected to a cost–benefit calculation. The costs are considered to be high, even for wanted, healthy offspring, while the benefits lie in the future. Infants not seen as able to provide a return on investment in the future are devalued:

> In Salic law [of the Franks in the sixth century CE] . . . one who killed a free young woman of childbearing age had to pay 600 sous . . . it is astonishing how small a case is made for the newborn, since the one who killed a male baby only had to pay 60 sous (30 sous if it was a girl).

Taken together, we have a diverse and extensive collection of factors that lead humans to treat each birth with trepidation, suspicion, and anxiety. So many, many things could go wrong. Hence, one can detect an attitude of detachment toward the newborn. If the child survives, it will form an emotional bond with its mother and she with it. Attachment is inevitable. Yet we shouldn't be surprised to find that cultures create models for "proper" behavior vis-à-vis the infant that actively discourage the formation of too-close ties. A principal element in such models is the notion that the infant is not yet fully human. I will review such models in the next essay, "Babies Aren't People."

Babies Aren't People

In the previous essay, I shared the results from a recent literature survey of anthropological studies of infancy. I identified six factors that typically cloud a newborn's future, ranging from uncertain paternity to parasitic infestation. If the fate of the majority of babies was in doubt, it follows that the community into which a child was born might be reluctant to make a deep emotional investment until the child's viability is confirmed. Most societies do not automatically confer personhood upon the newborn. Instead, the child is considered to exist in a liminal or intermediate state between a spirit world and the world of the living. In fact, it is very common to create a kind of external womb for the newborn—denying its birth. Here are three examples of the phenomenon (all referenced in D. F. Lancy, "Babies aren't persons."

In H. Keller and H. Otto, eds., *Different Faces of Attachment: Cultural Variations of a Universal Human Need* (Cambridge: Cambridge University Press, 2014)):

- "For the first three days of life the [Sikkimese Lepcha] baby is considered to be still in the womb and all the pre-natal precautions have to be observed. It is not even referred to as a human child; it is called a rat-child."
- "The new-born [Serbian Vlach] child sleeps tightly swaddled in a wooden rocking cradle which is enveloped from end to end in a blanket, so that he lies in a kind of dark airless tent."
- "the post-partum [Japanese] child remains, inseparably, a part of its mother. The infant continues to develop within the protective, womb-like environment of its mother's presence, excluding others."

Delayed personhood is accounted for in various ways and we find several folk theories that explain why this happens. "Not yet ripe" is one such theory. The denial of personhood is based on the patent deficiencies of the infant as a social being. Various attributes are singled out, including, for example, the infant's softness and lack of motor control. Significantly, these folk theories are not only used to explain the basis of nonpersonhood, but also include prescriptions for turning the babies into persons; they have "directive force." For example, the extremely widespread use of swaddling or cradleboard to restrain the infant is seen as compensating for and minimizing the long-term effects of the infant's softness and lack of motor control. Heat, smoke, massage, and special foods also "harden" the baby, as illustrated below (all referenced in Lancy, "Babies aren't persons"):

- "During its first . . . months the babe is considered highly vulnerable to danger from local spirits. Infant mortality among rural Javanese is in fact high . . . *slametan* [rituals] for the child follow at regular intervals during childhood, each accompanying a ritual event that introduces the child to a new, more secure stage in life."

- "Asked why infants are swaddled, [Afghani Nurzay] women explained that the newborn baby's flesh is *oma* (lit. unripe) like uncooked meat, and that only by swaddling will it become strong (*chakahosi*) and solid like cooked (*pokh*) meat."
- "[Northern Congo Azande] mother and child are both secluded after birth . . . at the conclusion of this period a feast is held. The child is brought out of the hut and is passed through the smoke of a specially prepared fire of green leaves . . . the child is not named by its parents nor is the midwife paid until it is certain that the child is hale [strong and healthy]."

Other areas singled out as needing ripening to transform the infant into a human being are speech, self-locomotion, acquisition of social knowledge and skills, and intelligence. Interestingly, there is relatively little consensus regarding the age at which personhood is achieved. This could range from a few days to eight or ten years.

- "not until the *kulio* (from *kungh* + *li*, lit: head shaving), on the eighth day after birth, does the [Malian Mandinka] infant move into the status of a fully recognized member of the family."
- "An [Angolan Ovimbundu] baby is born pink and it is only when he turns dark at the sixth or eighth day that he shows the first indication of becoming a person (*omunu*). He shows further promise in that direction with his first show of sense, but all through childhood he is . . . only a potential person."

In a strict statistical sense, the most common rationale for withholding personhood is that the infant itself has not yet committed to being human. It is suspended between two worlds, the human world and the "other" world of spirits, ghosts, ancestors, and gods. There are several variations on this theme. In one version there is a distinct tension between the spirit or soul and the body (examples referenced in Lancy, "Babies aren't persons"):

- "Having just come out of the Dreaming, the soul or spirit (*kurunpa*) of [Aboriginal] Anangu infants is still closely linked up and in communication with the Ancestors."

- "The perceived relationship of [Sierra Leonian Mende] infants with the world of spirits . . . generates loyalties in conflict with the world of the living . . . infants are presumed to develop unusual powers of vision and the powers to move across different sensory domains."
- "A newborn [Amazonian Yukui] has been contaminated by [puerperal] blood and is also more likely to succumb to disease or birth defects during these first few weeks of life. The baby was therefore regarded as not yet belonging fully to the world but lies somewhere between the spirit domain and that of the living."

Families aren't necessarily passive in the face of the infant's liminality. In the Bolivian Andes, a precise and elaborate swaddling procedure guards the infant against *susto*, an illness that results in the separation of body and soul. A caretaking style that emphasizes keeping the infant in a coma-like state—always quiet and sheltered—is also often justified on the basis of ensuring that the spirit doesn't flee. Of course, this policy (along with using swaddling and cradleboards) also reduces the amount of attention that the mother must devote to the infant. Further examples of proscribed procedures for securing the infant to the world of the living are (both referenced in Lancy, "Babies aren't persons"):

- "a new-born [Punan Bah—Malaysia] child is considered little more than a mere body of blood, bones and flesh. Only gradually, as the soul . . . takes up residence in the child, does it become human . . . The souls of children . . . can easily be scared away, and children must be handled with the greatest care at least till they are about four years old when they become more secure. [For example,] they are never punished physically so as not to scare off their souls."
- "General or prolonged fussiness, a refusal to eat or outright sickness—all these may be diagnosed as symptomatic of the spirit's withdrawal from the body. To secure its permanent integration with the body, the [Qiqiktamiut—Inuit] family and others make every effort to encourage it to remain[, including] the maintenance of a congenial atmosphere . . . and the creation

of important ritual ties to members of the community outside the natal household."

A point made earlier was that high infant mortality (among other factors) led to an emotional distancing between the newborn and its family. We have several lines of evidence from the way in which infants and children are treated in death that strongly reinforce the delayed-personhood argument. First of all, burial rites and mourning may be minimal or actively discouraged in the case of a child younger than five years, or even as old as ten. The attention of the family and community should be on the next child, not on the one who's died (following cases referenced in Lancy, "Babies aren't persons"):

- "It is not unusual for the [Amazonian Ayoreo] newborn to remain unnamed for several weeks or months, particularly if the infant is sickly. The reason given is that should the child die, the loss will not be so deeply felt."
- "[When a North American Chippewa infant died] weeping was frowned upon for the fear that the sorrow would be passed on to the next child."
- "when a [Tongan—Polynesia] child died before it was named, there was no mourning for no shades were involved . . . the old women will tell the mother to hush her wailing, saying this is only a ghost (*cello*)."

When we turn to the archaeological record, excavators often find that infants and children are buried apart from older children and adults. Specific examples follow (all referenced in Lancy, "Babies aren't persons"):

- "In Xaltocan [Mesoamerica] . . . burials of infants and young children less than four years of age were recovered from . . . under room floors and . . . also incorporated into house walls."
- "An analysis of Etruscan child burials in Tarquinia enables one to conclude that the absence of children below the age of 5.5 years from the principal cemeteries was suggestive of a major shift at that age."

- "[Argentinian Mapuche] infants are not buried in the cemetery, but are buried in the old family plot or somewhere near the house; it is believed that it would be harder for the child to be turned into a demon if it is closer to the house."

To sum up the survey to this point, it seems that it is only with the dramatic decline in the rate of infant/child mortality and the conversion of children from chattel to cherubs that newborns are now considered fully human. We reinforce this sense of humanity by giving a permanent name at birth, by making regular eye contact and using baby-talk or "motherese." Our newborns start life "owning" various items of value: their own room, high chair, crib, eating utensils, and entertaining toys. More than this, we now celebrate the "innocent" and "cute" infant, and attempt to prolong this cherubic state. As Cross notes, "Modern adults not only [cultivate] the cute 'look' and encourage cute behavior in children, but, in many cases, cultivate cuteness in themselves." Elsewhere and in the past, adults acted as if the baby was on probation and that its survival was uncertain. Furthermore, the baby's lack of the distinguishing human traits—bipedal locomotion, speech, motor control, and the control of elimination—signaled its not-yet-personhood. The child had to earn its humanity, usually through the aid of various prophylactic procedures and by passing certain milestones or rites of passage. In the next essay, I will discuss another set of folk theories of infancy that emphasize the baby's potential for good and evil.

Devils or Angels?

Earlier in this chapter, I suggested that, contrary to contemporary anxiety about adequate attachment between a mother and her newborn, the more pressing issue in many societies is to resist forming strong emotional ties to a creature who may not survive to become a useful family member. I described this dilemma as "detachment parenting." In the essay "Babies Aren't People,"

I explained that, in most societies, newborns aren't considered persons; the conferral of humanity may be a prolonged process as the infant/child demonstrates its viability, normality, and utility.

In this essay, I explore further the idea of delayed personhood. The most common view of the infant is that she or he is in an intermediate or liminal state suspended between *two worlds*. The infant is vulnerable because of the tenuous connection between its body and soul, but also quite potent in having the power to connect quite directly with the "other" world. Children can serve as conduits or magnets for forces that may be evil or good. A "two-worlds" folk theory not only explains the nature of infancy but also prescribes actions to be taken by the infant's caretakers. Among the Nzebi in Gabon, twins are seen as spirits who chose to live among humans. It is important not to offend them so they do not engage in reprisals, such as the communication of various diseases and bad dreams, or simply return to where they came from. More generally, ritual activity persisting into adolescence controls the malevolence, and eventually makes the child fully human. A caretaking style that emphasizes keeping the infant in a coma-like state—always quiet and sheltered—is also often justified on the basis of ensuring that the spirit doesn't flee. Further expressions of the two-world theory follow (all referenced in Lancy, "Babies aren't persons"):

- "A [Mandok—PNG] newborn's inner self (*anunu*) was not yet firmly anchored inside its body . . . and for this reason both new parents observed many food and behavioral taboos after the birth . . . New fathers were prohibited from going fishing in channels and in deep water, nor could they hull out canoes, carve, or chop down trees . . . If the child cried inexplicably, the Mandok believed that one of the parents had violated a taboo that caused its *anunu* to leave. A ritual specialist was then called in to "call the baby back." As the child grew, the Mandok believed that the *anunu* gradually moved from "the surface of the skin" to the inside of the body, a common belief in other areas of Melanesia as well."

- "[In rural Japan] the *Ubugoya* was a place where the mother and the baby could hide themselves from ghosts and evil spirits ... A baby was considered to be transferred into the human world by a god. A midwife ... played a religious role in guiding the baby from the gods' world to the human world and giving social recognition to the baby as a member of the community."
- "When the [Azande] child is born the soul has not become completely and permanently attached to its abode. Hence it is feared that the soul may flit away and this is one of the reasons for confining infant and mother to a hut."

On the other hand, as long as the child retains its ties to the spirit world, this access can be exploited. These innocent and pure spirits can be utilized to appease or otherwise communicate with the other world of ancestors and gods. Child sacrifice was not uncommon. In an example from the ethnographic record, the (Congolese) Bolobo believed that a bewitched adult could be saved by exchanging his/her soul with the uncontaminated soul of an infant. As the adult gradually recovers health, the infant sickens and dies. Other examples from antiquity include the following (all referenced in Lancy, "Babies aren't persons"):

- "children were seen to possess this particular gift and were considered to have a position intermediate between the human world and that of the gods ... Children were considered suitable for the task of prophesy, functioning as intermediaries between the divine and human worlds in Greco-Roman society."
- "[There's an old Japanese] saying: 'One of the gods until the age of seven' ... Before seven, children were weak, and could die easily from sickness ... they could instantly return to the world of the gods and Buddhas at any time ... possess the power to transmit the will of the gods ... and often played the role of medium between gods and people."
- "The classical and biblical texts, as well as archaeological study, all indicate that healthy living children were sacrificed to the

gods in the Tophet [sacred precinct] ... The burned bones found inside jars from the Carthage Tophet provide conclusive evidence for Phoenician child sacrifice."

- "[Roman] children had long been used in religious and propitiatory ceremonies, because of the quality of purity often associated with children."

- "Another consideration is that as long as the child's spirit acts as a free agent, it co-mingles with harmful spirits. [Aborigine] babies ... were vulnerable to attacks by *mamu* ... evil spirits that live in the bush. When an infant was bitten, his soul would fall ill.

Ironically, it is not a big step from the pure and innocent angel to the corrupted devil. The child may be viewed as threatening, either in its own right or as a vessel or avatar for ghosts and evil spirits. Further examples follow (all referenced in Lancy, "Babies aren't persons"):

- Protestant and Catholic dogma influenced the inclusion of infants within cemeteries. Newborns were considered to be corrupted by the original sin of their conception, and unbaptized or stillborn infants were not permitted burial in consecrated ground.

- "[Certain] births coincide with the intensely active and aggressive phase of the yearly *yin/yang* cycle, thereby imbuing the nature of such neonates with these dangerous traits ... Han histories suggests that parents who believed these predictions typically abandoned or killed ill-omened children rather than attempting to 'transform them.'"

- "They did not consider infanticide itself an immoral act. The basic reason for this was the newborns are categorized as inhuman. Consistent with the perception that birth processes are repulsive and dangerous, Korowai [West Iriyan] say that a newborn is 'demonic' (*laleo*) rather than 'human' (*yanop*). People explain this categorization by noting that a newborn's skin is uncannily pale, that newborns are torpid, and that their bodies are generally freakish."

- "The belief [in the Middle Ages] that infants were felt to be on the verge of turning into totally evil beings is one of the reasons why they were tied up, or swaddled, so long and so tightly."
- Echoes of these beliefs can be detected in the prevalence of monstrous children as the chief protagonists of so many "horror" movies.

"Attachment theory" and its descendants have created a narrative of infants "at risk" of emotional maladjustment. In my survey of sources from cultural anthropology, history, and archaeology, this perceived risk is absent. *It is to be presumed that infants' emotional needs are met simultaneously with their need for sustenance and nothing further need be done.* The survey also reveals that an alternate narrative identifies attachment, rather than attachment failure, as the risk. A strong emotional bond is seen as impeding a process whereby infants get pragmatically sorted into categories of wanted versus unwanted, timely versus untimely, legitimate versus illegitimate, strong fighters versus sickly ghosts, innocent versus demonized, and dealt with accordingly. The risk of inopportune attachment is met by an overarching cultural model that denies the newborn personhood, often until it is several months, if not years, old. Personhood is delayed until the child's spirit and body become firmly united and the individual "ripens" into an independent and unique being capable of social interaction.

With the decline in infant mortality, abandonment, infanticide, infant sacrifice, and models of changelings and other malevolent incarnations of the infant, we should expect that restraints on infant attachment or bonding will be relaxed. And that is certainly the case. But we must treat the practices associated with attachment parenting as serving the needs of *both* infant and parents. If they do not, then they should be abandoned or never adopted in the first place. There's no cause to see co-sleeping, on-demand nursing, constant contact, parent–child play, and face-to-face "conversations" with the infant (to name a few practices) as natural and essential for the child's well-being. These practices are unevenly distributed cross-culturally, utilized (or not) for pragmatic ends—infanticide a case in point. The contemporary environment, considering birth rates, health, and nutrition issues, has created an entirely different—and much more favorable—climate in which to nurture children. In fact, it wasn't until well into the twentieth century that the idea took hold that babies might be "cute" rather than either angels or devils. The environment, overall, is so favorable now that following the attachment-parenting credo is unnecessary and should be treated entirely as "elective." Babies fared poorly in the past, taking a back seat to the more pressing needs of their families. Having so dramatically enhanced the odds in the infant's favor, we must not let the pendulum swing so far that other family members, or even the very fabric of family life, must suffer to stave off the dubious threat of reactive attachment disorder or its doubtful kin.

"Baby Parading": Childcare or Showing Off?

In his original formulation of "attachment theory" in the early 1950s, Bowlby did not identify the father as a key player in the infant's becoming "securely attached." But times have changed. In the neontocracy, the child's "needs" become—for many parents—all-consuming. The Fatherhood Institute assigns the father a major role in the child-rearing process and warns on its website,

> A baby or child who feels confident that his/her needs will be understood and met by a caregiver develops what is called a "secure" attachment to that caregiver. When the infant or child does not feel confident in the caregiver's support, the attachment is insecure and this causes distress to the child.

While the contemporary cultural ideal for child rearing now includes the father as a necessary contributor, this has rarely been the case in the past, or in other cultures. In the entire ethnographic record of hundreds of societies, I'm aware of only two (Trobriand Islanders and very small bands of Central African forest foragers) where the father, willingly, plays a significant role in infant care. Indeed, we find many examples in the ethnographic record of outright father–infant avoidance. Fathers may, however, contribute to the upkeep of their children, and women are attracted to men who project a nurturing attitude toward children. In spite of the scarcity of evidence for childcare by fathers, we have found a number of cultures where anthropologists have described a scene in which fathers engage in brief, very public nurturing of their offspring. I've labeled this behavior "baby parading." But is baby parading about childcare or does it instead signal mate quality?

When anthropologists describe family life in village settings around the world, fathers and children are rarely found in the same context. They may not even reside in the same dwelling. Among the Na, in southwestern China, women and their children live in consanguine (all members are biologically related) households; children never learn who their fathers are.

The physical distance between fathers and their offspring may be ratified by custom. Societies construct elaborate rationalizations for the father's absence from the nursery. Kwara'ae "men's degree of interaction with infants was limited by beliefs that urine and feces were polluting." The infant's skin was also considered potentially polluting until it reached full pigmentation. Other societies consider it taboo for a father to pick up an infant. In the Highlands of Papua New Guinea there is the notion that a baby will die should the parents live together, because it may drink the father's war magic (contained in semen) with its mother's milk. Indeed, exposure to the gaze of a man who has "strong" war magic is believed to kill the newborn.

Social change also affects the father–child relationship. Employment opportunities associated with modernization bring new costs and benefits for village children and their mothers. John Bock and Sara Johnson collaborated on a sophisticated natural experiment to study the impact of Botswana fathers on their children. They compared children of migrant workers with children of fathers resident in the village. They reasoned that since the former were unable to enjoy the benefits—if any—of direct father involvement, the children should show a decrement in traditional skill acquisition compared with their peers. No such decrement was found. Generally, studies have failed to find evidence that the father makes much difference to the survival of children.

So what about "baby parading?" As we examined cases of father involvement in the ethnographic record, we found quite a few like the following (all referenced in D. F. Lancy, *The Anthropology of Childhood: Cherubs, Chattel, Changelings*, 2nd edition (Cambridge: Cambridge University Press, 2015)):

- "Among the Eipo [of Papua New Guinea], fathers pick up their baby at the women's area and carry it . . . for half-an-hour or so, getting friendly attention."
- "[Chippewayan] men are often seen walking around the village carrying their small children."
- "His [Fijian—Melanesia] father does not play with him often, but occasionally he takes the child on his back to attend a meeting or to visit a neighbor."
- "When an Ngandu [Central African] father holds his infant in public, he is 'on stage.' He goes out of his way to show his infant to those who pass by and frequently tries to stimulate the infant while holding it. A man showed me a large fish he had just caught and asked me to take a photograph of him with his fish. He promptly picked up his nearby infant, and proudly displayed both fish and infant. His wife was also nearby but was not invited into the photograph."

Other, similar examples come from Indonesia, West Africa, Oceania, Papua New Guinea, and North and South America. Since these baby-parading episodes were brief—terminated abruptly at the first sign of the child's fussiness or elimination, by the father passing the child back to its mother or usual caretaker—it seems clear their actions weren't about caring for the child or relieving its mother. A corollary observation is that male caretakers tend to carry the child in a precarious or temporary position (on shoulders, in the crook of the arm, held out in front of the torso), whereas women tend to tuck the child away in some carrying device on the back or hip. Men's carrying style is suited to short duration and maximum exposure, women's to comfort and protection. It could be argued that the purpose of baby parading might well be to make a conspicuous display of a man's suitability as a mate, either to prospective wives (in a polygamous society) or to lovers.

So do we see echoes of these findings in contemporary society? Absolutely. For example, in Sweden, legislated time away from work is available to fathers. They "are expected to be as capable and interested in active caretaking of offspring, including infants, as are the mothers. This 'soft' (*mjuk*) side of manhood has affectionately been called the 'velveteen-daddy phenomenon.'" But Sweden has not seen a drastic change in parental responsibility. "Women continue to be the primary parent. Men, as fathers, assist them." Japanese fathers, whose work and leisure keep them from home, were not expected to participate in the lives of their children. Indeed, many seemed to suffer from *kitaku kyofu*, an "allergic" reaction to their own homes. However, a concerted effort by the Japanese government to encourage men to become more involved in childcare, and reward them for it, is changing the culture.

Numerous recent studies in the West affirm the following generalizations: in highly educated, two-income families, men are doing more of the housework and childcare than they did in the past (near zero). However, they are doing less than they think they are; after the birth of a child, parents' housework increases, but the increase for wives is 40 percent more than for their husbands. A somewhat surprising finding is that mothers as well as fathers are spending more time in childcare than they did fifty years ago. This is likely due to the shift toward a more child-centered culture.

The following anecdote, from a study in the USA, vividly illustrates what La Rossa has called the "asynchrony between the culture and conduct of fatherhood":

> Sandy's and Ben's images of fatherhood were quite different. Ben thought about the new baby much as an athlete might think about a trophy: after it has been won, it sits on the shelf to be viewed from a distance. Sandy thought about fatherhood in much more

personal terms and imagined an active participant in Kim's childhood. When the baby arrived and Ben walked away from his responsibilities, Sandy's illusions about Ben began to crumble.

Still, the appearance of fatherhood coaches and a growing cadre of stay-at-home fathers suggest a significant shift in the role of father. It is no longer sufficient to be a "good provider"; a "good" father must also be "engaged" with his children. This tectonic shift in attitudes seems to be driven by at least two factors. One is the increasing participation of women in the labor force. Second, fathers are gradually joining the neontocracy.

Regardless of how involved they may become in childcare, men are only too happy to advertise their nurturing capacity by parading their babies in public. A *New Yorker* cartoon shows a well-dressed man approaching a park entrance. Outside the entrance stands a shady-looking character with a pair of strollers, each holding a child, and a sign which reads: "Stroll a Kid ... $10 One Hour, $6 Half Hour." The implication is that the well-dressed man might rent a child to parade his value as a potential mate. Baby parading appears in a range of popular media—from the first episode of the animated film *Ice Age*, to the sitcom *Cheers*, to automobile commercials. And studies show it probably works: the baby parader is more attractive to the opposite sex. For example, in a US study of mate attractiveness, female college students were shown photos of young men in various poses, including getting into a sports car and interacting with a child. Those shown with a child were rated as more desirable marital partners.

While the ideal of father involvement may not yet match the reality, we must remember that the very idea that fathers should be deeply involved with their young offspring, and serve as a mirror of the nurturing mother, is extremely recent even in highly educated social groups. Changing habits and beliefs, rooted in evolution and operative for tens of millennia, takes some time— even with growing consensus on the desirability of such change.

4   Children Playing and Learning

Across cultures, with very few exceptions, early childhood is a time for play. Parents may vary in how positively they view this activity, but, at a minimum, they see its value for keeping kids busy and out of the way. Toddlers are supervised during play by explicitly delegated sib-caretakers, with adults in the vicinity alert to the sounds of trouble. However, virtually all scholars who've observed children at play in village settings cite a wealth of opportunities for learning the culture. And many would agree that play is a "form of buffered learning through which the child can make ... step-by-step progress towards adult behavior." I argued that learning through play was more efficient than learning from instruction for several reasons, not least because instruction is often boring to the young, while play is arousing, and because instruction "requires an investment by a second party, the teacher."

From my earliest fieldwork in the Liberian hinterland bush, I was struck by this enduring phenomenon—children are active, hands-on, engaged learners. And a great deal of their learning occurs in the context of play. Even when physically inactive, they are intently watching what the adults are up to, gathering material for later make-believe scripts. In the next essay, I describe boys watching from the periphery as a court case unfolds in the town chief's open-air courtroom. While watching, the boys discuss the case *sotto voce* and the chief offers up frequent homilies that lift some mundane element in the case to the level of moral imperative or customary practice. The boys absorb all these lessons, as evidenced by the re-enactment of the court drama in their make-believe play later on. A key element in the watching, discussing, and re-enacting is that it is entirely child-initiated. This is one "classroom," among many in the village, where attendance is optional and there are no quizzes.

This laissez-faire attitude on the part of the elders regarding "teaching" children is consistent with four widely held beliefs about children. First, children want to learn their culture, so they strive for competence. Second, they learn best without adult direction and at their own pace. Third, they are motivated to learn useful skills in order to "fit in" and be accepted by their families. And fourth, expecting children to strive to "fit in" means that when they appear to lack this motivation, they will be called to account. In the chief's court, "fitting in" meant being quiet and not interfering. Contrast these views with our own beliefs that children learn little without teaching, and need to meet certain specific age- or grade-determined milestones in their learning. Nor are they really required to "fit in" as their parents give them a free pass—to the despair of their teachers.

As the essays in this chapter illustrate, within tightly defined limits, parents may accord autonomy to children—to acquire and use a large library of interactive media or to choose from a self-constructed menu of food offerings, as examples. But unlike the villagers anthropologists study, their lives are, otherwise, tightly managed, including their play.

Cowboys and Indians and the Origin of the Couch Potato

Many years ago, I undertook an ethnographic study of childhood in a remote West African village called Gbarngasuakwelle. Ethnography is the method used by cultural anthropologists. It involves living with the people they're trying to understand; speaking the local language; learning and respecting their customs; and, above all, observing and listening, recording faithfully what is heard and seen, then trying to make sense of it as a nonnative. One of the prominent themes in my report (published as *Playing on the Mother-Ground*) was the importance of observation in the lives of children. As just mentioned, one venue where I hung out was the town chief's court.

With apologies to fans of Court TV, the average court case is just slightly more interesting than watching grass grow. And this was certainly true of the local court presided over by Chief Wolliekollie. Imagine a forty-minute debate about the failure to *promptly* return a borrowed lantern, or an even longer debate over the amount of compensation appropriate in the case of an adulterous liaison (the *juicy* details discretely glossed over). And yet the court never failed to attract a good crowd of juvenile spectators. While the boys watching the chief's court were quiet and blended in with their surroundings, it was obvious that the chief saw them as "pupils" in an open-air classroom. His rhetorical questions and judicial "opinions" often reflected basic principles of Kpelle morality. Most societies are keenly aware of the child as voyeur and fully expect to use public events for their didactic value.

Among the Yakutat of British Columbia, "Children learned a great deal by listening to the older people talk, especially when the old men gathered in the sweathouse to bathe and chat." Among the Tale of Ghana, "children learn who their . . . ancestors were by listening at sacrifices." Anthropologists note that little is private or off-limits to children in the village, and they learn about the birds and the bees quite early. For example, Australian Arunta children play at being husbands and wives, making separate windbreaks and fires and pretending to cook food. Sometimes they also play at adultery, with a boy running away with the "wife" of another boy.

So one of the first clues an anthropologist might note as evidence of children's autonomy to learn on their own is that the culture is displayed like an open book. There is no censorship and children can browse at will. In contemporary society, we seem to embrace a philosophy of "do as I say, not as I do." Because we focus so narrowly on children learning through explicit lessons, we ignore the many lessons we teach without intending to. Sociologist Peter McClaren recorded this scene some years ago:

> Georgette and Wendy picked up some dolls at the activity center. Georgette chose G.I. Joe and Wendy picked up a Farah Fawcett doll. "Let's pretend we're married," Georgette said. "Okay," Wendy agreed. Georgette took G.I. Joe and promptly slapped the Farah doll across the face with it, shouting: "That's what you get for talkin' to me like that."

Years after recording the African scenes of children as spectators, I had an epiphany and realized that what I had witnessed in Gbarngasuakwelle was the fertile field in which couch potatoes might grow. It turns out to be a small step from watching interesting things happen in the village, to watching television. In the village, however, the court case eventually ends and the juvenile spectators disperse for new, usually more active, adventures. By contrast, in many contemporary homes, the television/video game/iPhone is never off. While village children's prolonged and intense observation and eavesdropping on adults may be vital in learning their culture, interest is bound to fall off once they've "mastered" particular aspects of the "curriculum." Older boys do not hang around the court; it is all too familiar. The boredom that comes with overfamiliarization and lack of challenge is all too common in our classrooms, in contrast to the perpetually novel and challenging interactivity found in contemporary recreational and social media. Unfortunately, attempts to hybridize academic content with video game interactivity have not been notably successful.

Boys in Gbarngasuakwelle were also enthralled by their elders' success in hunting and trapping, and spent countless hours in chasing games and "play" hunting that evolved into the real thing. In my childhood, I was a cowboy. I grew up without a village; my windows on the world were books and television. But I didn't become a couch potato either. As exciting as those Saturday morning westerns were, I took equal or greater pleasure from *replicating* the heroic exploits of the Lone Ranger or Hopalong Cassidy. My parents could not afford, nor did they approve of, building a toy treasury for me. But they believed that fantasy play stimulated the imagination, and contracted with Santa one year to provide me some "props," including a cowboy hat and six-shooter. We do, occasionally, see village parents supplying cast-off or scaled-down tools and weapons as toys, to encourage children to use play as a learning medium. Even more important is the belief that, while playing and learning outdoors, children are distracted and don't get in adults' way.

This is a belief my mother shared. So I spent hours each day "roamin' the range." In the process, I remained lean and healthy, and hence, according to Nigel Barber (blog = *The Human Beast*), would have more easily evaded predators in an earlier incarnation during the Paleolithic.

In contrast, television and video games, and the comfortable environment in which they are situated, may be so compelling that the child never shifts from observation to replication. Couch potatoes not only miss out on physical exercise, but may be shortchanged in their mental exercise as well. In fact, there are numerous studies showing a strong inverse correlation between time spent with video games (current average = thirteen hours a week) and school grades. So parents may need to intervene (minimally) to nudge children from passive receptors to active creators and, above all, to get them off the couch and into the backyard or the neighborhood at large. Recent studies highlight how few families spend any time at all outdoors in leisure activity in the typical week. "Children not only don't wander through their neighborhood playing with peers; three-fourths of them don't even play in their own backyards." Parenthetically, on the subject of toy guns and modern derivatives, many child advocates worry about the impact of violent video games on aggressive behavior. And this is one parental anxiety that is justified. A thorough survey of the huge literature on the relationship between violent video games and later aggressive behavior found that the "evidence strongly suggests that exposure to violent video games is a causal risk factor for increased aggressive behavior, aggressive cognition, and aggressive affect and for decreased empathy and prosocial behavior." At least some of these negative effects may be due to diminished face-to-face (see the "Gamesmanship" essay below) social interaction that is associated with children who are absorbed in media for hours on end. That said, if children use guns to harm or kill themselves or others, the culprit is far more likely to be the careless gun owner who often justifies ready access to a lethal weapon by the need to "protect" themselves and their family. Virtually any day of the week in the US one can find a minor news item of the "Boy, 4, shot by sibling while waiting in car" variety.

What can we take away from all this? Children are endowed with several predilections that facilitate their learning culture with little or no direct instruction. Those predilections can still be useful today in helping a child learn to construct narratives (stories) and to learn many aspects of the culture. However, in the village there is no lens through which the culture is distorted on its way to the child's brain, except for their own naivety. But if electronic media represent the window *our* children have on society and history, it is "through a glass darkly." Product advertising dominates the cultural "lessons" conveyed. Other "lessons" seem almost anticultural, gaining their audience through the egregious violation of cultural standards and mores—think *The Simpsons*. In the village, common "child-produced" content emerges in make-believe play in which children take pride in replicating the skills and pursuits of those older. In contemporary society, child-constructed narratives may be telegraphic, barely literate prose, sexting, and cyberbullying.

Toys or Tools?

Archaeologist Bob Dawe was intrigued by a puzzle. His field is the prehistory of the Plains Indians, which he reconstructs from studying early sites that were utilized by these people. Many of the sites contain the remains of large mammals that were hunted as a staple of the diet. These "kill" sites include buffalo jumps, where large numbers of animals were killed and butchered. Among the bones are the tools used by hunters, including stone arrow points. The puzzling thing is that these often include large numbers of small, poorly knapped arrowheads that would have made no more impression on a bison than a mosquito bite.

Dawe's hypothesis is that the points were quickly and crudely made to give to children, who would use them in "toy" arrows. He buttresses his argument with material from ethnographic studies and travelers' recollections. Many observers of the Plains Indians (including John James Audubon) took note of adults giving children scaled-down tools—especially for hunting—which they were expected to use to gradually perfect their skill. Dawe writes, "Toys should not be considered nonfunctional. Rather they are small-scale tools which functioned and suffered the same tool use-life as their adult-sized counterparts."

While not universal, in many societies tools are made for children to play with and/or they are given cast-off tools to convert into toys, and/or the raw materials to make their own. Franz Boas—one of anthropology's founding fathers (and mentor of founding mother Margaret Mead)—described how Inuit (Eskimo) boys played a game that simulated the hunting of ringed seals through the ice. The materials used in the game, such as pieces of sealskin and miniature harpoons, were often supplied by parents to encourage this kind of learning through play. Similarly, Inuit "girls make dolls out of scraps of skin, and clothe them like real men and women. Their mothers encourage them, for it is in this way that they learn to sew and cut out patterns." Girls from the Conambo tribe in Ecuador will, as their mothers before them, become potters. While quite young, they can be found playing with balls of clay donated by their mothers. They turn the clay into snakes, miniature animals, and hollow vessels, all baby-steps on the way to learning to produce useable ceramics. In a Chiga farming village, a small child is given a gourd to play with, to balance on his/her head and, trailing after older siblings, takes it "to the watering-place . . . brings it back with a little water in it."

Even more common, I've found many cases where children are free to handle and play with adult-sized tools. Most striking are children literally "playing with knives," a few examples of which follow (all referenced in D. F. Lancy, "Playing with knives: The socialization of self-initiated learners," *Child Development*, **87**, 2016):

- "[An Amazonian Pirahã child] was playing with a sharp kitchen knife, about nine inches in length. He was swinging the knife blade around him, often coming close to his eyes, his chest, his arm and other body parts, when he dropped the knife, his mother—talking to someone else—reached backward nonchalantly without interrupting her conversation, picked up the knife and handed it back to the toddler."
- "[A Tanzanian Hadza] infant may grab a sharp knife, put it in its mouth, and suck on it without adults showing the least bit of concern until they need the knife again."
- "'I don't like it when our children play with machetes, but if the baby decides to play, I leave it. And if the baby cuts themself and if they see the blood, they themselves will decide not to play with the machete.'" (Aka (Central Africa) mother)

Appearances to the contrary, I do not think this nonchalant attitude reflects indifference or callousness toward the fate of one's children. Rather, this extreme laissez-faire attitude reflects a bedrock belief in the power of children to learn autonomously. More than this, parents often express the view that parental intervention of any sort, including teaching, is a waste of time (children will learn without it) and may even be harmful if children become reluctant to explore and learn on their own. This "folk" wisdom was recently confirmed in a series of experiments, undertaken by psychologists in the US, using a multi-action toy. Four- and five-year-old subjects "who were taught a function of the toy performed fewer kinds of actions on the toy and discovered fewer of its other functions" than children who were not taught anything about the toy.

Village children not given toys made by adults, or not finding any full-scale tool available, make their own. These constructions often display enormous ingenuity, persistence, and skill. An unusual case is found in Kutch, where Rabari boys start their education in animal husbandry by creating a "flock" out of dried camel and sheep droppings, and then moving the flock, corralling it, taking it to water, and so on. I have observed dozens of toys

Figure 4.1. Bara boys playing with clay figurines they've made

that were created from recycled materials, many quite elaborate, such as wire cars or trucks made throughout Africa. Even when toys have no obvious connection to useful skills or knowledge, children may learn a great deal through the *process* of invention and construction. I was enthralled by a youngster during a trip to Yemen. He had scavenged a cast-off plastic jerry can, modified it to use as a sled, and proceeded to launch himself, repeatedly, down a stone parapet.

Figure 4.1 shows a pair of boys from the Bara tribal area of south central Madagascar playing with clay figurines they've made themselves. The author of the photo, Gabriel Scheidecker, writes,

> The boys are playing with vehicles made from clay. The toys are modeled after *sarety* (borrowing from French charrette, ox cart) and mainly used for transporting the harvest (rice and manioc). The toy versions are called *kisarety*. The prefix ki- signifies small, not serious, and is used for all children's games and toys that reflect adult activities/things. The boys have "loaded" one cart with "rice" (sand) pulled by a Zebu (note the hump) ox. Humans are depicted with their arms bent in a way that suggests they may be engaged in an "ox fight."

In 2010, I visited a Vezo fishing village in southwest Madagascar. The community depends, for its livelihood, almost entirely on collecting marine resources. From adolescence, villagers will venture out into the Zanzibar channel in colorful outrigger canoes to fish and hunt turtles. The wide expanse of beach fronting on the sea—from which these expeditions are launched—serves as a kind of mixed-age, teacherless classroom. Babies are placed in tide pools to splash around and grow accustomed to saltwater; three boys around age five clamber over a beached canoe, learning an agile dance from thwart to gunwale; six-year-olds convert discarded planks or logs into "canoes" they ride on and paddle. The first lesson in sail-handling probably occurs as the boy maneuvers a miniature sailboat he has made himself. In short, a significant part of the "canoe curriculum" can be acquired through play with "toys."

Am I suggesting that *our* children be given free rein in the garage, workshop, barn, kitchen? Hardly, but most parents and teachers could widen the safety zone for them and provide many more opportunities to explore and learn independently. My own childhood was greatly enriched by having many opportunities to "build" things with cast-off construction materials, using my father's tools—unobserved by an adult. Ultimately, I'm not sure which practice is more harmful for children—playing with knives or the opposite. A Korean-American journalist remarked, "I was surprised in the United States when a nine-year-old asked me to butter his bread because he wasn't 'allowed to use a knife,' even a butter knife."

What lessons do *our* children learn from toys? It could very well be that they are primarily learning to be avid consumers. In my view, "Black Friday" is aptly named. It is a black day on the nation's calendar. A few years ago, while watching the nightly news, I was treated to a horrific scene of a crowd bursting through the doors of Toys "R" Us. I watched as a cute blond cherub got knocked down in the crush and, for all I know, trampled. The announcer's commentary—completely upbeat—extolled the social and economic benefits of this phenomenon, ignoring the anarchic behavior on the screen. One study relevant to my question looked at "Dear Santa" letters in the UK versus Sweden. The latter bans television advertising aimed at children, the former offers no such prohibition. The results, unsurprisingly, showed that British kids had longer wish lists and requested primarily "branded" toys. Another study in Britain reported, anecdotally, about eleven-year-old Philip, who was particularly pleased on his birthday because his auntie had followed his directions and made the right choice. He proudly declared, "I wanted a Huffy [scooter] because they're the best at the moment and so I gave her the product code number and price and everything in case she got it wrong." Eric Clark has reviewed these studies and notes, sardonically,

> Kids get bored with their toys before they break them, sometimes even before they have played with them. In fact, many toys are no longer created for play. They are designed to be purchased, to be possessed, to be a badge of status. The more toys, the happier the child. A survey in 2005 showed that 80 percent of children under 12 were given more than 10 toys a year, but 60 percent of those toys were soon thrown out even though there was nothing wrong with them . . . For most toy companies, the role of children is clear: they are cash cows to be milked.

It turns out that childhood observers saw this coming from a long way off. In a history of American childhood, published in 1917, the author laments, "two days playing with [contemporary toys] exhausts the pleasure. They are too complete—the fun of making them has been taken away from the child."

Whatever lessons are being learned, they are different lessons. Historian Gary Cross charts the steady decline in popularity of construction sets and other toys that can serve as tools. As he says, "Toys that prepare children for adult life seem harder to find." Five years ago, Stinky the Garbage Truck was hot. I noted three salient attributes of this toy. First, it was expensive (seventy dollars) but available at a discount. Second, and lamentably, it promised to fill the void for a friend- or siblingless child. "Who could believe a trash-gobbling garbage truck could be SO love-able? There's a ton of fun surprises in store with your new pal: Chats, joke telling, exercise partner and sing-along silliness, too. Friendship with Stinky™ never smelled sweeter!" But Stinky's central lesson seems to be that toys are trash: "He can 'eat' garbage. [And the] garbage your child feeds him can consist of anything from other toy cars to several tiny toys your child is sure to have lying around his or her room." By 2015, it was passé and no longer in production.

Unfortunately, manufacturers of traditional, sturdy, creative, and constructive toys have not fared well. My favorite company, now deceased, was Back to Basics Toys. Instead, children and their parents seem to prefer toys that come with a narrative already provided (via television, video games, or commercials). But I'm being overly pessimistic. Fine construction toys are still made (although I'd buy the more generic Lego block set over the single-purpose "movie-themed" sets). Lincoln Logs is celebrating their 100th anniversary. Venerable board games like Monopoly still have valid lessons to teach, including the meaning of "friendly competition." Most of the tools of the domestic kitchen are harmless and should be accessible to children, especially when they want to "help" make dinner. The same is true for garden tools. Parents and prospective parents may need to re-examine their leisure time—first by increasing it! Can one's hobbies be selected with eager-to-learn children in mind? Cooking? Gardening? Sewing? Volunteering at the Humane Society? Taking up a musical instrument? Learning a foreign language? How about the "urban farming" movement? Williams Sonoma has lovely chicken coops ranging from $300–$1,500.

Gamesmanship

In his study of "moral" development, the great Swiss psychologist Jean Piaget observed children of different ages playing marbles, and used the game to illustrate the child's passing through

numerous stages before arriving at a mature (fully moral) understanding of social conventions.

In watching players, we first see the refinement of manual
dexterity. Humans are tool users, and young humans, as a consequence, are object manipulators. In its most refined form, using
perfectly polished and round orbs, playing marbles calls forth
tremendous small motor skill and digital finesse. Then we see
"gamesmanship," where children manipulate the rules and each
other to enhance the quality of play as well as their own success.
Lastly, we see the development of social understanding, of an
appreciation of rules qua rules.

By at least the Roman era, and probably earlier, children used
knucklebones as projectiles to try and dislodge each other's sta-
tionery targets. In other words, the basic pattern of marbles—
whereby a player shoots a hard object at one or more similar
objects to drive it, or them, out of a demarcated area—is probably
quite old. Marbles, as we know the game, is clearly shown in
Breughel's 1560 painting *Children's Games*. In Adriaen van
Ostade's *Children and Dog* from 1673, boys are playing marbles
outside a tavern. More recently, I have found marbles (and its kin)
being played all over the world.

Renowned British folklorists Iona and Peter Opie document
three basic versions of the game, but the variation in rules of play
is staggering. What was critical, from Piaget's perspective, was
that the game could be played at various levels so that very young
children might play, even without understanding most of the
rules. He wrote, "Children's games constitute the most admirable
social institutions. The game of marbles, for instance . . . contains
an extremely complex system of rules, that is to say, a code of
laws, a jurisprudence of its own." After documenting the primary
dimensions of the game, Piaget begins to probe the players'
cognitive representation of the rules.

> You begin by asking the child if he could invent a new rule . . . Once
> the new rule has been formulated, you ask the child whether it could
> give rise to a new game . . . The child either agrees to the suggestion

or disputes it. If he agrees, you immediately ask him whether the new rule is a "fair" rule, a "real" rule, one "like the others," and try to get at the various motives that enter into the answers.

Piaget teases out distinct age-dependent styles in children's approach to marbles. Initially the child plays with the marbles as interesting objects, but there's no game per se. By about age four, the child can play the game, knows how to make the right moves physically, and understands the necessity for turn-taking. "The child's chief interest is no longer psycho-motor; it is social." He is able to imitate the model provided by a more mature player, but he really has no sense of strategy or of what to do to increase the likelihood of winning. Then, around age seven, players focus on winning, even though their grasp of the rules—as revealed through questioning—is still vague. By age eleven, the child is an expert on marbles and can explain every rule and exception. Nevertheless, the child still hasn't grasped rules qua rules. He still sees them as immutable. But, by thirteen, boys understand that the rules are arbitrary and conventional.

There are hundreds of illustrations of children's games from history and anthropology. Unfortunately, relatively few describe children actually in the process of playing, as opposed to a dry catalog of the rules and mechanics. But we can make a number of generalizations from the descriptions that are available. First, because toddlers are usually under the care and supervision of their older siblings, games are flexible enough to permit their participation. Older, more expert players will *handicap* themselves, for example, to ensure that learners can enjoy some success. Complexities in the rules are introduced gradually. Games are played in a neighborhood playgroup of mixed age and gender. "Winning" is far less important than maintaining amicable relations. Players, in their roles as child caretakers, do not want the cries of an unhappy charge to attract the scrutiny of an angry adult.

The playgroup is hardly awash in a constant flow of good feelings, however. We have vivid accounts of protracted arguments about rules and their application. Particularly in the groups of older children—which tend to be homogeneous with respect to age and gender—games are not so much about learning and adhering to rules as about a running exercise in negotiation. As the Opies document for marbles, and Candy Goodwin for hopscotch and jump rope, there is a constant alteration between individual attempts to gain an advantage, cries of "foul" by opponents, and negotiated agreements that permit the game to proceed. Collectively, I've referred to these diplomatic skills as "gamesmanship."

In many cases, games support particular cultural ends. Aymara boys in the Andes play marbles—girls play jacks—while herding their flocks far from the village. Ben Smith's careful description of these games complements his in-depth analyses of speech and social-interaction patterns during play. Smith discusses the importance of *qhincha* (bad luck) in marbles. By confronting and enduring *qhincha* in the game, boys successfully fend off accusations of being feminine or homosexual. By implication, a boy who keeps control of himself when something goes wrong (a pebble in the path deflects his shot, say, or a toddler tramps through the ring of marbles) demonstrates the "chacha-ness" or "toughness" that reflects masculinity.

The very ethos of the culture may dictate the nature of play. In the emerging Israeli state, the kibbutz was created as a utopian alternative to the competition and status differentials inherent in Western society. Not surprisingly, a study of children's games revealed a bias toward egalitarian outcomes—no winners, no losers. In Oceania, one finds examples of societies that are so egalitarian that, in children's play, "Competitiveness is almost never in evidence." Among the Tangu of Papua New Guinea, children in teams play a game called *taketak*, which is designed—in keeping with local values—to end in a tie.

In small-scale, band societies, the playgroup, necessarily of mixed ages, must allow all players, no matter how inept, to participate; the playing field is always level, so to speak, and supports the prevailing egalitarian ethos. !Kung children throw a weighted feather in the air, and, as it floats down, they strike it with a stick or flick it back up into the air. The "game," called *zeni*, is played solo, and children make no attempt to compare skill or success. Aka foragers are highly egalitarian, and Boyette notes the absence of rough-and-tumble play and competitive games. *Ndanga* is a popular game in which "there is no winner in the game and there is no score kept."

In contemporary, middle-class, Western society, marbles and similar amusements are rapidly becoming extinct. The Opies blame this decline on the rise of adult-managed games and sports, but we might also cite video games as a major factor. Should we be at all concerned about this? Is a fondness for old-fashioned games purely sentimental? I don't think so. As opportunities for children to "negotiate" through rule-governed play dwindle, scholars are increasingly excited by the possibilities of Machiavellian intelligence (MI). There is a revolution under way in our thinking about the *sapiens* part of *Homo sapiens*. One useful starting point is Richard Byrne's *The Thinking Ape*. He writes,

> the essence of the Machiavellian intelligence hypothesis is that intelligence evolved in social circumstances. Individuals would be favored who were able to use and exploit others in their social group, without causing the disruption and potential group fission liable to result from naked aggression. Their manipulations might as easily involve co-operation as conflict, sharing as hoarding.

The theory has garnered a steady stream of empirical support. Extrapolating from it, I would argue that, if children have Machiavellian brains and, further, that brains need to be exercised to fully develop, marbles and the like are the perfect mental gym. The key elements here are rule-governed play, flexibility in applying the rules, and an absence of adult umpires. That is, children must be free to construct successful gaming sessions without adult guidance or interference. That's the essence of gamesmanship.

Unfortunately, current child-rearing practices have largely expropriated the opportunities for children to exercise gamesmanship and MI through unsupervised play. Adults now thoroughly manage and script most children's activities. Gary Fine's

Figure 4.2. Team players

ethnography of Little League has become the definitive study of adult-managed play. He notes that the official Little League rule book ran to sixty-two pages in 1984 (and to 100 pages as of 2009) and that, in dramatic contrast to games organized by children, in "Little League, negotiation by players is unthinkable." Indeed, when players attempt to protest an umpire's call, for example, coaches and others call them "unsportsmanlike."

In addition to adult management of what were once child-initiated games and pickup sports, growing evidence indicates that parents—at least those among the contemporary intelligent-sia—are taking control of make-believe play as well. This recent change in the way parents behave arises from their attempt to fill in for the siblings and peers their increasingly isolated children do not have, especially in urban settings. Parents also seem to feel that a child's unguided play will not yield the kind of academic payoff that parent-directed play yields. And, importantly, parents fear their offspring may suffer physical or psychological harm if they play with "neighborhood" kids. Parents may view marbles as dangerous because a child might swallow and choke on one. Despite such worries and good intentions, curtailing play initiated by children seems likely to attenuate—if not destroy altogether—opportunities to develop the skills associated with gamesmanship. One unintended consequence, for example, may be the rise in bullying as children lose opportunities to nurture and develop the ability to bargain and argue their way through disagreements.

But we can fight back. For starters, we can weigh in on the debate regarding the overly academic atmosphere in many pre-schools and the shift toward a more play-based curriculum. We should get behind the drive to restore recess to the elementary-school program. Some school districts and municipalities hire playground or recess coaches "who hope to show children that there is good old-fashioned fun to be had without iPods and video games and [who'll help] students learn to settle petty disputes, like who had the ball first or who pushed whom, not with fists but with the tried and true 'rock-paper-scissors.'"

Social critics warn parents to allow children greater freedom, particularly in play. As evidence that further decline is not inevit-able, consider that March was declared Marbles Month at the Horsham Primary School in western Victoria, Australia. The game, school officials promised, would be vigorously promoted.

5   Protection versus Suppression

The theme of this chapter is the deepening conflict between protecting our children and smothering them. It is apparent to me that in acting on our increasing and unjustified paranoia about our children's safety from an array of extremely improbable perils, we are ignoring the far, far more probable harm we may be doing to their development as competent, self-sufficient, and successful adults. We are no longer protecting; we are preventing them from taking advantage of a plethora of opportunities to learn through experience.

For many years, I have idealized childcare and education in Scandinavia. During repeated visits, especially to Norway and Sweden, I have been very impressed by their insistence on granting children the freedom to explore, to interact with, and to learn from each other and the environment. When visiting preschools (free and practically mandatory) in Sweden, I was often told, "There is no bad weather, just bad clothing." And, indeed, every child is expected to play outdoors for lengthy periods each day wearing, if need be (often), sturdy and effective foul-weather gear. These play sessions are not managed, and only lightly supervised by adults.

So I was truly saddened to read a recent article describing drastic changes in Norway's official policy on government-run early-childhood education. First, the authors of the article present a thorough review of the relevant empirical literature, which finds widespread support for the idea that risky play can be extremely beneficial for children and acts as a kind of multipurpose vaccine to prepare children for life's vicissitudes. Specifically,

> Other benefits that derive from children's engagement in risky play are the lessons for life that they unconsciously learn while

they practice handling risks. Risky play, as several researchers suggest, helps children enhance their ability to master peril . . . children seek out thrills gradually in encounters with progressive risks that allow them to master comfortably the challenges involved . . . risky play has an anti-phobic effect on the fears and phobias (such as fear of heights, fear of water, and separation anxiety) . . . In spite of these benefits and in the absence of any evidence that Norwegian children are actually at risk from serious injury or abduction, the government has introduced restrictions to assuage parents' growing and irrational anxieties.

The authors then proceed to present the results of a large-scale survey of managers of early-childhood centers, which the vast majority of Norwegian children attend, without cost. The following are remarks made by these managers (all taken from E. B. H. Sandsetter and O. J. Sando, "'We don't allow children to climb trees': How a focus on safety affects Norwegian children's play in early-childhood education and care settings," *American Journal of Play*, **8**, 2016):

- "Climbing in trees is accepted but only up to a certain height and always with adult supervision."
- "We had to remove the swing due to rules regarding the safety zone. A play hut was removed because of the danger of pinches and the lack of a shock absorbing surface."
- "New rules on playground equipment define what is allowed in the institution's outdoor space. More creative equipment voluntarily built by parents, an old boat and ropes between trees, had to be removed . . . All outdoor activities must be approved. We have limited possibilities for building nature playgrounds with natural climbing and play equipment."
- "The local authority has removed all trees. Children are not allowed to climb. The major focus on injuries makes parents anxious and afraid of what type of activities their children are involved in, i.e., walking on slippery surfaces. We still do this . . . to teach children to handle different surfaces, but we have to consider this carefully and explain a lot to the parents."

- "The younger children can no longer be on the playground when large puddles have formed."
- "Sledding under icy conditions is [now] prohibited."
- "Children get frustrated over being stopped in 'dangerous' play. I'm afraid that this safety focus makes it more unsafe for children. They become less competent in mastering 'difficult' obstacles . . . the safety hysteria has resulted in a lack of physical challenges for children."

This trend is spreading rapidly, particularly among professionally employed parents with small broods of children. In the UK, researchers speak of "cotton wool kids" in describing children who are treated as being so fragile as to need a constant protective wrapping of soft, white cotton. Another study from the UK showed a dramatic decline in the last twenty years in the number of unaccompanied children permitted to cross the street, go to the cinema, or use public transport. Obesity is rapidly increasing, in part because parents consider it too risky to let their children "run around" the neighborhood. Neighborhood play is also discouraged because parents are concerned about children "getting in with the wrong crowd." Clarke notes that parents use toys as the means to compensate children for the withdrawal of freedom. Children forgo exploring their environment (many areas of the home are off-limits as well) in return for richly furnished indoor play.

In the US, the typical "recess" in the school day—designed to allow children to blow off steam in free play—has been eliminated, sharply curtailed, or now subject to adult control and management. These changes were motivated by exaggerated concerns for children getting hurt, teasing, or bullying each other, or getting abducted. Add these concerns to our increasingly litigious culture (true, particularly, in the US) and we find schools managing children's activities, not for their benefit or safety, but to stave off potential lawsuits initiated by overly protective parents.

The growing incidences of child asthma, eczema, celiac disease, and other allergies, as well as autoimmune disorders like diabetes, are now being blamed on our tendency to shrink-wrap our kids in a too-clean environment. We prevent them being exposed to bacteria-rich and tolerance-inducing dirt, manure, animals, and plants. Amish farm children in the US have far lower incidence of allergies than do non-farm children. Farm children encounter all sorts of generally harmless but immunity-building "bugs" as they carry out their chores. The typical suburban/urban child is "protected" from the need to work, and that includes most chores, which precludes gardening and animal husbandry. But dirt may be good for you!

Scientists explain the phenomenon this way: we are born with an immune system that is in "learning" mode for the first two years of life. The immune system doesn't "know" who its enemies are. If the infant is kept in a hyper-clean bubble, the immune system fails to get programmed. Ideally, as children play outside and with pets, they encounter novel but harmless substances— even those that might lead to an infection—and these prime their immune system so it will learn to sort out harmful bacteria from harmless ones. If the child is "protected" in hyper-clean environments, later, the "unprogrammed" immune system overreacts to things it should simply ignore, like cat dander, eggs, peanuts, or pollen, leading to allergies and asthma. Worse, the nondiscriminating immune system may turn on the body itself, leading to autoimmune disorders; attacking the cells we need to produce insulin (Type 1 diabetes), for example, or hair follicles (alopecia), or even targeting the central nervous system (multiple sclerosis).

> A century ago, more people lived on farms or in the countryside. Antibiotics hadn't been invented yet. Families were larger, and children spent more time outside. Water came straight from wells, lakes, and rivers. Kids running barefoot picked up parasites like hookworms. All these circumstances gave young immune systems a workout, keeping allergy and autoimmune diseases at bay.

Overprotection applies also to the child's emotional development. In school, teachers may be so anxious to protect the child's self-esteem that they shower them with praise and withhold appropriate negative feedback. Results may be the opposite of what is intended—frequently praised children lose motivation and persistence.

Where parents, historically, used threats of the bogeyman to restrain children's behavior, modern parents go out of their way to eliminate fears of "monsters" and such. Halloween—Dia de Los Muertos or All Souls Day—was, in the recent past, an opportunity for children to experience the supernatural, encounter fear, and take risks. Now, parents in the US acknowledge that Halloween is no longer "scary," recalling fondly the hijinks and excitement of their own unsupervised trick-or-treating. Twenty-first-century parents are reluctant to expose their children to "danger" or anything frightening. As an example, "A mother who took her child on a Halloween hay-ride 'which turned out to be scarier than expected regretted her decision.'" It's no surprise, then, that schools may ban costumes that are bloody or gory, and weapons (plastic!) as accessories. My neighborhood has embraced "trunk-or-treat," where mothers drive their costumed children to the church parking lot and dispense treats from sacks in the trunk of the car. Halloween has become just another occasion for a parent to make his/her child happy by willingly spending money on his/her chosen costume. Appropriately, it is now referred to as the "Orange Christmas."

Trick-or-treating at Halloween also evokes the widespread and irrational fear of child abduction. In the US, parents now take children to the local police station to be fingerprinted "in case." Now I find that *really* scary.

Parents seek to maintain children in a state of innocence and dependency as long as possible. Images of college students going to sleep clutching teddy bears suggests how successful they have been. Parents infantilize their children by overprotecting them and assuming them incapable of handling any challenge. In the interest of keeping children innocent, we are eager "to protect children from dirty words and pornography but not to shelter them from consumer desire." Students may also be protected from scientific information that runs counter to religious orthodoxy. This may be one reason why, by international standards, students in the US are scientifically illiterate.

Another overprotection opportunity arises when children are engaged in competitive play under an adult's direction. Colleague and mother of two Jennifer Delliskave weighs in:

> One of my biggest pet peeves about kids and playing games/sports is the current "everyone's a winner" philosophy. Case in point: several years ago, I had a birthday party for Liz. We played a couple of party games. At the end of the first game, I gave a prize to the winner. Several of the "losers" started bawling—loudly. I couldn't figure out what had happened. Through sobs, one of them asked me why they didn't all get a prize. When I said, "Because you didn't win," the kid bawled even louder. Shaun (Liz's father) had to go rummage around in a toy box to find little cheap toys to give the losers. They didn't even care what the prize was, they just wanted something. Doesn't teaching kids "everyone's a winner" (giving prizes just for participating) deprive them of learning how to be a "good" loser—how to be gracious? When I was a kid (and I know this applies historically in the USA & Europe), we were taught to congratulate those we lost to, and then figured out how to beat them the next time around—learning from our mistakes. Losing at various games/sports also taught me about my personal strengths and weaknesses (I'm not a professional softball player for a reason).

Jennifer's story suggests that parents are going to great lengths to ensure their child is never treated unfairly. I see this happening in the banker's precision used in allocating presents or rewards in a family with two or more children. Parents should consider two things before committing themselves to the goal of ensuring that their child never gets the short end of the stick. First, the world has sticks of all lengths and that's a lesson children should learn to deal with. Second, a grown-up child may very well accuse a parent, retrospectively, of "favoring" a sibling, and this charge may spring entirely from the individual's character. Some children/people are thin-skinned and readily feel slighted. It's just how they are. Trying to achieve complete equity across multiple siblings in the distribution of resources—including affection—might make things worse.

What is ironic and truly tragic is that while children of economically successful parents are overindulged—often to their detriment—an intolerable proportion of the world's children are growing up in a kind of living hell. In northern Nigeria, hundreds of children *have* been abducted and "sex trafficking" is a worldwide problem. Living in poverty, many millions of children are suffering the combined horrors of overpopulation, civil war, and terrorism, and a range of attendant health risks. The contrast between our lengthening of childhood (see the Chapter 7 essay "Failure to Launch") and the shrinking childhood in a world torn by suffering and strife is well represented by images of malnourished slave children in Côte d'Ivoire harvesting cocoa beans that will be processed into the chocolates consumed by obese children in the West.

In the following essays, I examine four different aspects of the overprotection crisis.

Nanny Angst

I live in the state of Utah, which ranks near or at the bottom in publicly funded support for daycare. Furthermore, the dominant Church of Jesus Christ of Latter-Day Saints (LDS), unlike churches in other parts of the country, does not make unused facilities available to daycare providers. Aside from an underlying fiscal conservatism, the failure to support daycare rests on notions of morality and on folk beliefs about child development. A typical homily goes:

> This divine service of motherhood can be rendered only by mothers. It may not be passed to others. Nurses cannot do it; public nurseries cannot do it; hired help cannot do it—only mother . . . can give the full needed measure of watchful care.

While the emphasis on children preferentially being cared for by their biological mothers is central to the LDS faith, it seems to me that many Americans share some version of this belief: childcare rendered by anyone other than the biological mother is bound to be less adequate, and the child's prospects, if cared for by someone other than the mother, will be diminished by some degree. The fact that these views persist, in spite of overwhelming evidence that the mother's employment and use of professional childcare are not associated with any measurable diminution in child welfare, suggests that they have deep roots in contemporary US culture. I hope to show that the "mother-knows-best" belief is just that—a belief—and it is not found very often either cross-culturally or historically.

In the remainder of this essay, I would like to contrast the view just noted with views or folk models found in other societies. First, all such models incorporate the idea that the entire extended family is responsible for childcare. The preferred caretaker (also referred to as an "allomother") is typically a grandmother or an older, female sibling. Grandmothers are considered especially appropriate caretakers for the newly weaned child, as they provide succor and stability at a time of emotional stress. In Botswana, it "is not uncommon for children to call their mothers '*sisi*' [sister] and their grandmothers 'mother.'" Indeed, scholars have argued that menopause creates a stage in the human lifecycle expressly to enable no-longer-fertile women to devote their remaining lifespan to the care of their grandchildren.

After grandmothers, older sisters are preferred as caretakers. In a comprehensive survey of the ethnographic record, Weisner and Gallimore found that 40 percent of infants and 80 percent of toddlers are cared for primarily by someone other than their mother, most commonly older sisters. No less a personage than Hillary Clinton claimed that she, "like many firstborn children, learned to care for children by baby-sitting my two younger brothers."

Figure 5.1. Sibling caretaker, Madagascar

While older brothers and fathers are less often involved with childcare, Barry Hewlett has documented some dramatic exceptions, especially among highly egalitarian foraging bands. Several other scholars have documented the great flexibility inherent in allomothering as babies and toddlers are, literally, passed around among extended-family members even for nursing.

Turning now to more complex societies, we see a transition among the upper class, or those who can afford it, from caretaking shared among family members to professional or extra-familial care. The role of wet nurse may well have a claim on the title "world's oldest profession," as indicated by the spectacular tomb of Maia, King Tut's wet nurse, discovered fairly recently. Wet nurses were ubiquitous in ancient civilization. In more recent history, one of the hallmarks of modernization and rise of a large middle class is the greater and greater emancipation of mothers.

sending infants out to nurse was one of the first luxuries women demanded ... experts of the day ... proceeded to advise on how to choose a nurse ... she should be healthy ... of a good disposition, since they believed that the milk somehow contained the nurses' personal traits. One biographer noted that Michelangelo's nurse was a stonecutter's wife, by way of explaining his interest in sculpture.

Wet nurses may have been the first in a parade of caretakers. Sculptures and paintings give us many clues to domestic life in ancient Greek and Roman societies. Graves have yielded thousands of small statuettes of women holding children; these represent the *kourotrophos* or nanny. The *kourotrophos* was preceded by a *nutrix* or wet nurse, and followed by a pedagogue, who protected the older child in public; took him to and from the gymnasium; and taught him proper dress, manners, and demeanor (high-class girls didn't leave the house). All these non-maternal caretakers had complementary roles to play in the child's development.

In the modern era, we can look to Europe, Scandinavia, and Italy, in particular, for a continuation and expansion of the shared-caretaking model. Sweden has perhaps led the way in creating an elaborate, state-supported structure to provide high-quality care, from birth. The child is allocated a fundamental right to the best care available, regardless of the income, time available, competence, and inclinations of its biological parents. This emphasis on quality needs to be noted because, in countries where the government does not impose appropriate standards on daycare providers, children may just be warehoused, and the only "developmentally appropriate learning experiences" are (more likely than not) provided by the television. Further, there is no evidence to suggest that all stay-at-home moms provide the intellectual fertilizer necessary to nurture their child's thought and language to support school-readiness.

In short, it is probably a fair statement that our emphasis in the US on the full-time ministrations of the child's biological mother is unprecedented in the annals of culture. We should not treat the employment of nannies, grandmas, and daycare centers as unfortunate, but sometimes necessary, deviations from the ideal, but rather as a continuation of childcare practices that have prevailed throughout most of human history. So to those who would lay a guilt trip on working mothers for their use of extra-familial childcare, I say, "back off." Undermining a mother's confidence and well-being through guilt and self-doubt is hardly conducive to creating a psychologically healthy environment in which to raise children.

Child-Proofing versus Tool Using

The argument made in this essay is that not only does much of our anxiety and overprotection of children seem unnecessary, but also we may be "protecting" children from valuable experiences. I will call attention to the striking contrast between how we think about child development compared to our ancestors. Undoubtedly, a key ingredient that makes a creature human (or chimpanzee, for that matter) is tool invention and use. Even though our distant ancestors were tool users, they used a single tool—a rather crude hand ax—virtually unchanged for more than two million years. So, in evolutionary terms, the explosion in toolmaking skill, the variety of useable tools and materials, and so on, occurred fairly recently—during the Middle Paleolithic about 300,000 years ago. From this period, and moving forward, archaeologists have found clues that suggest how children went about the business of becoming toolmakers and tool users. These clues emerge from the study of stone-tool manufacturing sites or "workshops." In these sites, there will be an area where the debris from toolmaking, and various unsuccessful or incomplete tools, lie scattered. Further analysis reveals distinct patterns showing the presence of toolmakers at various levels of expertise. Typically, an expert toolmaker—who provides a live demonstration of skill—is working in the center of the assemblage, perhaps near the open fire. Close by are the journeyman toolmakers, clearly competent but less expert, their mistakes and imperfect tools more common. At a further remove we can see the remains of children's tool-making efforts. Characteristically, the youngsters are working with poor-quality stone rejected by those more competent. Poorly made blade tools show evidence that the child had gotten the general idea, re tool shape and knapping technique, but "lacked the skill to complete it." This will come with more practice. Two inferences can be drawn from this line of research. First, children were welcomed at toolmaking sites, if they were mature enough to avoid disrupting the work of others. This afforded them ample opportunity to closely observe the experts. Second, it looks like they either found or were given practice material—stone of sub-par quality (which could be sacrificed), but still adequate for exploration and practice.

Another clue to how children become expert tool handlers is quite evident in the behavior of contemporary infants. As evidenced by crib mobiles, stuffed animals, teething toys, bathtub toys, and all manner of "approved" and "safe" objects made available to babies, we clearly recognize their proclivity for exploring and handling objects. Infants grasp objects as soon as they are able and wave them around, bang them on hard surfaces, splash them in water, and, above all, mouth them. This suite of exploratory behaviors is driven by the infant's need to make sense of the environment, and when you're largely immobile and can't see very well, ready access to manipulable objects is a good place to start.

The transition from handling objects, to learning their properties, to using them as tools, is almost imperceptible. It is a short step from exploring objects to attempting to do something with them. In a classic study, Connolly and Dalgleish carefully documented children's mastery of the spoon—perhaps the first tool to be used successfully by a child, at least in our culture. They made video recordings at monthly intervals of children aged twelve to twenty-three months. The skill of using a spoon appears to be built in a broadly similar way by different infants, in that the order in which the problems are addressed is the same. Initially, rudimentary actions with the spoon are observed; for example, dipping it repeatedly into the dish, banging it on the table, or putting it in and out of the mouth. These simple repetitive actions serve a number of purposes. They provide a means whereby the infant learns something of the mechanical properties of the spoon, and they also anchor the ends of the process. The launch pad is the dish with its food, and the destination is the infant's mouth. Significantly, the child persists at attempting to use the spoon over an extended period, gradually perfecting the skill; but until reaching complete mastery, he receives no reward for his efforts. No food finds its way to his mouth. Therefore it appears the child is *compelled* to master a skill which he sees others in his family using routinely. He seems equipped, by nature, with a suite of complementary motor movements that appear automatically over time. Parenthetically, I would suggest that the conscientious parent will not only ensure the child's nourishment in spite of their inability to feed themselves, but also enable the child to use and practice with the spoon—in spite of the mess entailed. That is, to learn to use tools, children must have opportunities to observe competent tool users and—as noted developmental psychologist Jerome Bruner pointed out— they must be able to practice with real tools.

But do we routinely meet this test? I don't think so. I believe that one consequence of the growing concern (bordering on paranoia, in some cases) for children's safety is that we have "de-tooled" our children's environment. For safety reasons, we have sequestered all the real tools in our homes and substituted wholly inadequate plastic replicas, such as the Black and Decker Junior Drill which can't actually drill anything (but parents are still warned that the toy represents a "choking hazard"). Not neglecting the aspirant cook, toymakers provide "realistic-looking" blenders, mixers, and toasters which can't blend, mix, or toast.

In contrast, my research has turned up a significant number of societies around the globe which not only do not tool-proof their children's environment, but willingly acquiesce when children ask for or take even the most dangerous tools. (The following are referenced in D. F. Lancy, "'Playing with Knives:' The socialization of self-initiated learners," *Child Development*, **87**, 2016.)

- On Okinawa, an anthropologist describes a four-and-a-half-year-old boy who secured a sickle because "there was no adult around to peel a long stalk of sugar cane . . . so, with expert strokes and handling of the razor-sharp tool, he shaved off the thick, hard skin. By the time his mother arrived on the scene, the child was busily chewing and sucking on a considerable length of the peeled cane."
- Amazonian Matsigenka "three-year-olds frequently practice cutting wood and grass with machetes and knives."
- Amazonian "Parakanã . . . young girls take a big knife and go into the forest in small groups; they cut green palm leaves and . . . weave . . . baskets (peyras)."

Figure 5.2. Matses boy practices chopping wood

The very common practice of permitting children access to real but potentially dangerous tools does not spring from indifference or callousness. On the contrary, these parents understand the child's powerful need to learn from and with the artifacts commonly employed by older community members. They acknowledge the child's need for autonomy so that she can learn the culture and, in particular, the helpful skills that earn the family's approval. Children do so willingly, but at their own pace and in their own way. (Think of the three-year-old angrily declaring "I can do it myself!")

While we've focused on tool using, the "freedom-to-learn" model applies across the spectrum of skill and knowledge. For example, children are extremely knowledgeable about forest products and their uses in medicine, building, basketry, and edibles; but to obtain this knowledge, they must be free to travel in the forest, usually with older siblings looking after and modeling for younger ones. Adults are rarely involved in these bush expeditions beyond giving children a kind of shopping list for products they need.

Now consider a contrasting case arising from our penchant for overprotection. In Christine Gross-Loh's best-selling *Parenting without Borders*, she reports, "I was surprised in the United States when a nine-year-old asked me to butter his bread because he wasn't 'allowed to use a knife,' even a butter knife." While we may exaggerate the danger posed by a butter knife, according to my editor and colleague, Jennifer Delliskave, we grossly underestimate the threats embodied in a young adolescent's access to a smartphone. This tool is easily mastered by young people without instruction. A brief story is in order. An art historian colleague of mine took her mother and fourteen-year-old daughter on a "culture" trip to New York City. The fourteen-year-old begged to be excused from museum visits so that she could remain behind in their hotel room to Instagram and text with her classmates. These were girls who were not actually her friends and seemed not to like her, according to her mom. Aside from being incredibly time-consuming, social media opens the possibility that the jealousy and rivalry among teens can become virulent and hateful (sexting, cyberbullying) without the checks imposed by the adult oversight available when these conflicts play out in public. It may be worth pointing out that cell phones without apps or text messaging are still available at a fraction of the cost of a smartphone.

My focus on the cross-cultural contrast in attitudes toward children and tools can readily be expanded to include virtually the entire culture. That is, in the village, the child engages directly with objects, processes, and scenarios that are on open display. The village and individual homes haven't been child-proofed. Children show great eagerness to learn and innovate. Their learning and work are usually embedded in a social context of family or peer activity, especially play. By contrast, in our society, the child's entire environment is managed and mediated by adults. Taking initiative, handling "grown-up" stuff, exploring beyond one's backyard, and finding new playmates, only occur "with permission," which is often withheld "for the child's own good." It is no wonder, then, that so many researchers studying modern family life report the complete absence of children's interest in learning on their own or volunteering to help out. On the contrary, "even school-aged children appear helpless, with parents assisting them in simple activities such as getting dressed ... and the routine inclusion of chores in children's schedules has generally fallen by the wayside in middle-class family life."

What Price Happiness?

> Plumbing the depths of children's desire [is now considered] good parenting.

Some years ago, a US newspaper story caught my attention. Michelle Cossey was arrested in the aftermath of her fourteen-year-old son Dillon's incarceration for planning a Columbine-style school massacre. When asked why she had purchased firearms which enabled Dillon to assemble what police called an "arsenal of weapons," the mother replied, "He was unhappy." Presumably her solicitation was also responsible for the boy's all-too-evident obesity. The case, fortunately, ended before anyone was killed, unlike the later Sandy Hook massacre.

Mercifully rare, the Cossey case nevertheless signals a problem of national significance—at least in the US—and I'm not referring only to gun deaths or school shootings. Parents' preoccupation with their children's happiness seems to be drawing a tidal wave of unintended consequences in its wake.

The idea that children should be happy and that their unhappiness should alarm their parents is not, by any means, common among the world's societies. After all, children are inarticulate, they are weak, they don't know much, their social status is very low, and they suffer from continual hunger and illness. Why *should* they be happy? As Heather Montgomery reports from her study in a Thai village, there is "no concept of any golden age of childhood . . . children are pitied because . . . they are everybody's *nong* (younger sibling/inferior)." For Ifaluk islanders, conspicuously happy children are a cause for concern and may require chastisement. Children are usually fed last and rarely given toys or presents. During weaning, the child's distress is particularly evident, but its tearful entreaties and tantrums are usually ignored.

Historians note similar sentiments expressed by early writers on childhood. An archbishop in the late Middle Ages promised damnation for parents who might "serve their children like idols!" In the sixteenth century, early childhood was described as a period of unalloyed misery due to high infant mortality, chronic illness, the child's dependency on others, lack of fluent speech, and its inherent sinfulness and general uselessness. However, it should be evident that tearful episodes and bouts of unhappiness inevitably give way to good cheer and mentally healthy adulthood. Indeed, Charles Dickens, in *Dombey and Son* (1848), expresses the widely held view that "childhood, like money, must be shaken and rattled and jostled about a good deal to keep it bright."

Exaggerated concern for the child's happiness is thus a fairly recent idea which seems to be growing apace. Parents who take

Figure 5.3. Pair of children from Papua New Guinea Highlands

their children abroad are quick to discover how thin-skinned they are. Youngsters suffer severe culture shock as they are exposed to the rowdier interactions of their foreign peers. Especially in Japan, children are toughened through rough physical play, endurance training, and mutual teasing, according to US academic Daniel Walsh, whose kids were pushed around but, ultimately, benefited from their encounter with Japanese peers.

I'm not suggesting that children develop best in a state of misery, but our assumption that children's natural state is one of continual bliss, and that any departure from this state requires remediation, has led to a host of unintended but quite damaging consequences. These include the epidemic of child obesity (and accompanying need for blood-pressure medication) brought on by indulging the child with snacks while accommodating their avoidance of active play or the out-of-doors. Heeding the unhappiness alarm has resulted in a tripling of youth on anti-depressants since 1993, and preschoolers comprise the fastest-growing psychiatric-drug-using demographic in the United States.

Our responsibility for our child's happiness extends well into adolescence, as titles like *Queen Bees and Wannabes: Helping Your Daughter Survive Cliques, Gossip, Boyfriends, and Other Realities of Adolescence* suggest. And while we readily accept that parents should meddle in their teenagers' social lives, Alexandra Robbins's recent exposé, *The Overachievers*, and reactions to Amy Chua's book, *Battle Hymn of the Tiger Mother*, suggest that parents who encourage and facilitate their children's need for achievement are suspect. Even though there's no evidence that high achievers are at risk, Robbins would have us quail at the possibility of the potential emotional damage should these "overachievers" topple from their lofty perches. On US college campuses, personnel—from dorm monitors to faculty to coaches—are besieged by "helicopter" parents flying (or phoning) to the aid of their unhappy and evidently helpless offspring.

In the US, we tolerate mediocre academic performance and rail against teachers who expose our children's failings. Schools in Connecticut have banned teachers from using red ink. Others are encouraging teachers to grade papers in "more pleasant-feeling tones," such as purple. These initiatives are part of a massive campaign to protect children's "fragile" self-esteem, a campaign that persists in spite of overwhelming evidence that, if anything, high self-esteem is associated with academic failure—especially among African-American students. And, more recently, a large-scale study found that students who are indiscriminately praised, and denied accurate feedback on their performance, lose motivation and persistence.

The social cost of inflating self-esteem may be reflected in several recent Cassandra-like reports decrying the poor international standing of US students and the growing gap between the academic achievement of high-school students compared with the requirements of the college curriculum.

I think it is time parents reconsidered their assumptions about children's "natural" state. Should we expect them to wear a permanent smiley face? Might they be better off, especially in the long run, to experience the states of hunger, cold, frustration, failure, and the pain of a scraped knee? Is being "picked last" the same as being bullied? Should their wish list be our shopping list? Must we monitor and strive to adjust their popularity, worry whether their clothes are in fashion, or insist that their teachers acknowledge their "specialness?" Perhaps we might practice a little more "benign neglect." Go ahead; try it. They'll thank you later on.

Turning *Inside Out* Inside Out

Should we take comfort from the blockbuster film *Inside Out*, or is it a prophesy of bad things to come?

Inside Out is one of those films that all my friends—who are more avid movie-goers and review readers than I—insisted, "You must see it." So I did, but only after it was available at the Redbox kiosk. It's not that I dislike animated films, Pixar's in particular, but I had a really bad feeling about this film after reading a couple of reviews and seeing the trailer. This, in spite of the accolades the film had earned: Oscar for "Best Animated Feature" and box-office receipts approaching a billion dollars. My trepidation arose from what, for me, was the central message of the film: "Riley needs to be happy." Aside from her anxious parents—she's an only child—Riley, the film's tween protagonist, is surrounded by a team of emotional bodyguards whose sole occupation is to assure that she is never unhappy.

Before turning the film inside out, I need to set the stage. First, I'm an anthropologist, and as such I don't believe that any human behavior can be understood strictly as a psychological or bio-logical phenomenon. Culture plays a profound role in organizing the way we understand things like a "normal childhood." That is, what is "normal" and "good" in one society may be seen as aberrant, strange, or even harmful in another society. Our society in particular has been called out as an extremely "weird outlier" and, hence, one of the worst subpopulations one could study for making generalizations about "normal" behavior.

The basic message of the previous essay was that the postmodern society we live in is one of the very few in the world (and in recorded history) that is committed to the idea that children's normal state is happiness, and that any deviation from that state commands intervention.

Our children are free from any responsibility for maintaining the household, caring for younger siblings, or supplementing family resources. These are all part of the routine chore menu for less privileged children in history and around the globe. Corporal punishment—virtually taboo in the West—can, in earlier times and other cultures, be expected following failure to carry out these responsibilities. I could extend this list of threats to a traditional village child's happiness almost indefinitely, but the amazing thing is that anthropologists, sometimes with surprise, consistently report that village children are exuberant, active, playful, and happy.

Trying to vaccinate and protect the child against unhappiness may have negative consequences. For one thing, the more society projects the mandate of perpetually happy children—a complete myth, according to Firestone—the greater the likelihood that even small breaches of this nirvana will provoke unhappiness and even serious mental illness.

Another and very serious threat arising from this obsession with child happiness is thoroughly discussed in Frank Furedi's book *Therapy Culture*. Here is a sampling of his remarkable insights:

- "If children as young as four are seen to be legitimate targets for therapeutic intervention, it is not surprising to hear of a growing demand for expanding such services for babies. In the USA, infant mental health has become an established professional specialization."

- "The belief that there is a deficit of the elementary emotional attributes required for child rearing, and that, therefore, third-party therapeutic intervention is called for in the parent and child relationship, is a widely held assumption of parenting 'experts'" (resulting in a tripling of youth on antidepressants since 1993).
- "Recently, the Archbishop of Canterbury has claimed that therapy was replacing Christianity in Western countries. According to Archbishop Carey, 'Christ the Saviour' is becoming 'Christ the counsellor.'"
- Furedi sees "a decline of an ethos of public responsibility and the sacralisation of self-absorption. Contemporary culture continually promotes the ideal of fulfilling your own needs and the primacy of expressing yourself. Feeling good becomes an end in itself—and the individual relationship to a wider moral or political framework threatens to become an insignificant side issue. Questions of right and wrong become arbitrary matters to a devotee of the cult of feeling. Instead of right and wrong, there are only different ways of feeling about the world."

And now, the film. The action takes place on two stages. First, we see (animated) scenes in which Riley grows from toddlerhood to preteen in the protective care of her middle-class family and lifestyle. For example, at the appropriate age, Riley begins to participate in the almost obligatory organized team sport—in Minnesota this is ice hockey. The second stage is inside Riley's brain. This is an extremely colorful world—in fact, the aesthetic I would describe as Toys "R" Us for five-year-olds or Barbie's Xanadu. And the characters inhabiting this world are of a piece—diminutive, but with relatively large heads and very large eyes. Incidentally, this trait of prolonged juvenile appearance is called "neotony" and is thought to provoke a positive, nurturing response from others.

As I mentioned, the team populating Riley's brain is there to aid in making her happy. Think of them, collectively, as akin to "snowplow parents" who remove all obstacles and detours in the child's life course. They manage Riley's emotions via a freestanding "console" much like a DJ's (very large) music mixer. JOY is the happiness manager. She is in charge of the console, keeping Riley happy all day long.

The "FEAR" character's main role is to keep Riley safe—constantly on the lookout for potential disasters. FEAR's brief is easily recognized by the growing legion of critics who think parents are overprotective. He is constantly evaluating the possible dangers, pitfalls, and risks involved in Riley's everyday activities. There are very few activities and events that FEAR does not find to be dangerous and possibly fatal.

ANGER feels very passionately about making sure things are fair for Riley. He has a fiery spirit and tends to explode (literally) when things don't go as planned. ANGER also comes to Riley's aid in a hockey game.

DISGUST is highly opinionated and her job is to protect Riley from being polluted by her surroundings, especially her peers. She wants to make sure that people won't taint Riley with their toxic behavior or bad clothing advice. She wants to keep her from being in any situation that's uncool. The role of DISGUST is played in the real world by mothers in Wiseman's *Queen Bees and Wannabes*.

More minor characters continue the theme of protecting Riley. Bing Bong is Riley's imaginary friend and, unlike real friends, Bing Bong never competes with Riley, teases her, or says something unkind. He remains innocent, childlike, and safe. The FORGETTERS are in charge of removing unnecessary and unpleasant memories from Riley's memory store.

SADNESS is a bit of an anomaly and one wonders what she's good for, as the whole point seems to be to prevent Riley from ever experiencing negative emotions. Fortunately for her, SADNESS is redeemed in the end when the team discovers that a soupçon of unhappiness/sadness may actually be good for Riley, helping her through a crisis.

Everything runs according to plan for the first eleven years of Riley's very happy life, but then her father takes a job in San

Francisco. Riley gets her first exposure to cacophonous, gritty urban life. In short, San Francisco is the real world and Riley, having spent the first ten years of her life in a kind of cotton-candy cocoon, is clueless and vulnerable. Her team is acutely aware of Riley's unhappiness, as are her miserable parents. The resolution of Riley's unhappiness crisis involves the team (SADNESS, in particular) coaxing her into "seeking help" and "expressing her feelings." This provokes the necessary understanding and succor from her parents, helping Riley to accept that not feeling happy 24/7 may not be the end of the world. But, just in case, the five Emotion Managers get a larger, more complex console to better help Riley as she copes with many more threats to her happiness quota (e.g. puberty).

As upbeat as the film is, I can take no comfort from its message. Unfortunately, I think it reinforces an unhealthy trend toward increasing children's dependence and vulnerability. This growing paranoia about unhappiness in children may be eroding much of the resiliency, persistence, and toughness that they are endowed with from birth, and which is critical for later success and well-being. I think the movie tries to convey this message at the end with the idea that a little sadness can be healthy, but it is too little and too late to reverse the mostly dysfunctional themes.

6   Going to School

I'll begin with the tale of the clueless snowboarder. For quite some time, my radar has become more and more attuned to a scenario where a family is on vacation in unfamiliar surroundings. Aside from parents, there's at least one child, let's say nine or older. Of course the family has to decode their surroundings to find destinations, master novel forms of transportation, consult signs and a map, make sense of the street grid or trail signs, and so on. While the parents are actively engaged in this process, the child grows impatient and, eventually, asks a question or questions with, if only she/he too had been using her/his powers of observation and analysis to make sense of the situation, self-evident answer(s). As I noticed and paid attention (I myself am a frequent and avid traveler) to these scenarios, I began to have an epiphany.

This epiphany crystalized for me on a ski outing. As a skier, I am fortunate to live in a state which justifiably claims to have "the greatest snow on earth." We have many ski resorts and, in turn, they have many ski-lifts. These are, with one exception, either chairlifts or gondolas. Using either of these lifts is a no-brainer. Not so with the single exception: a "Poma" lift at Powder Mountain Resort—an old fashioned, low-volume lift that was common fifty years ago. As my wife and I waited for our turn on the Poma, I noticed a group of four teenaged male snowboarders ahead of us. They were deeply engaged in an animated conversation. As they edged forward to the loading point, one of their number, who'd had his back to the lift while chatting, took the lead, slid over to the mounting point, and then looked around frantically and emitted a plaintive "How do you do this?" The lift operator reluctantly came out of his warm hut and conducted an impromptu lesson. The boarder did not succeed on his first try or his second, or third. In fact, five Poma units climbed the hill without a rider while those in line fumed.

The clueless snowboarder had at least five minutes in line to closely observe the mounting procedure. He might have encouraged his more experienced mates to precede him so he could watch their technique and seek their advice, but he didn't. Aside from the rather self-centered and asocial aspects of the young man's behavior, it reveals something else. I would argue that—with the exception perhaps of electronic media—young people have lost the motivation for, or even the skill of, learning independently through observation. Alison Gopnik reviews a large and recent body of experimental research comparing children's learning and exploration under the guidance of a teacher versus self-guided learning. She concludes: children's attention to "what the teacher wanted . . . made them worse at actually learning."

From my admittedly limited research, it seems that children have become almost wholly dependent on lessons as the means to learn new ideas and skills. As unfortunate as this may seem, it may be inevitable. As on so many issues discussed in this book, parents seem to be operating on the principle that if a little bit of something (toys, food and wardrobe choices, adult–child play, protection from harm, extracurricular activity) is good for kids, then a lot of it will be even better. Yes, there is evidence that some academic preparation in some areas is very helpful. But how much is enough and how much is smothering? "Conscientious" parents now create lessons for babies. Many are devotees of "Baby Signs" where speechless infants are trained to communicate in a version of ASL. These parents explain their appreciation of Baby Signs (all taken from L. Acredolo and S. Goodwyn, *Baby Signs: How to Talk with Your Baby before Your Baby Can Talk* (Chicago: Contemporary Books, 2002)):

- "We have used this book with both of our sons. Our oldest (now three) has a vocabulary more than most five-year-olds. Even our pediatrician commented on his vocabulary skills. But all of this is secondary to just being able to meet the needs of our kids. We know if they are hungry, tired, thirsty, or need a diaper change."

- "My son is only twelve months old . . . and he talks better than most two-year-olds. Hurray for Baby Signs!"
- "Considering how slowly babies learn even easy works like *ball* and *doggy*, let alone difficult words like *scared* or *elephant*, many months are lost that could be spent having rich and rewarding interactions, both for the child and the parent."

At the other end of the lifespan, we see a spectacular increase in the use by *adults* of *personal coaches* for all manner of self- and professional improvements, in lieu of self-guided learning. I don't think this parallel is a coincidence.

I want to argue in this chapter that there are processes implicated in contemporary schooling that are, in a sense, "unnatural." Our forebears did not rely upon teaching, texts, and classrooms to prepare children to become successful adults. So the roles of "student" and "teacher" must be learned. Not all who embark on this path are successful. Currently, especially with the growing importance of standardized testing, we seek explanations for the "failure" of students and teachers. But if the ethnographic and historical records are treated as a baseline, we should, rather, be seeking to explain successful cases, since they are more improbable.

Clearly, parents contribute to success by engaging the child in academically oriented activities such as reading and mature, intellect-stretching conversation. Like any other parental intervention, however, academic preparation can be overdone. Too much of the wrong kind of at-home pedagogy is as likely to turn kids off schooling as turn them on. We don't want children to become conditioned to the idea that learning is only acquired through lessons. The world doesn't need more clueless snowboarders. Instead, the parent who wants to cultivate his/her children as curious discoverers of knowledge should be alert to any spark of interest that can be subtly fanned into flame.

I am heartened whenever I meet a child who's crazy about dinosaurs. This passion has two very positive attributes. One, the child is learning on its own, without supervision or lessons. Two, the child has perhaps discovered that, in becoming an "expert," he/she is acquiring social capital. Not everyone understands the peculiar anatomy of the Stegosaurus.

The Resistant Scholar: Don't Blame Teachers, Schools, Curricula, or Television

Currently, in the US, we spend a king's ransom on efforts to improve the performance of schools, teachers, and students. These costs incorporate lengthy programs of training for would-be teachers; individualized plans and curricula for "challenged" students; modern school facilities, including the latest in digital technology; very costly mass testing; and complex systems of evaluation and reward or remediation. In spite of rising investment in both public and private schools (and hybrids), "report cards" reflecting outcomes such as readiness for and timely graduation from college are more likely to indicate failure than success. However, I'm not going to sink a shovel into well-ploughed ground. Instead, I want to offer a fairly novel perspective on this issue, drawn from work on how children learned before there were schools and from the history of schooling over the millennia. That history is instructive, but unfortunately it does not suggest that any of these ambitious programs will turn around our reluctant scholars.

Camilla Morelli has been a recent participant observer—with a focus on children—in a transitional community of Matses Indians in the Peruvian Amazon. She marvels at how facile and active the Matses children are in the natural environment, compared to her own feelings of ineptitude. She is cowed by three- and four-year-olds who competently paddle and maneuver dugout canoes on the wide river. She observes young boys nimbly catching and handling enormous catfish. And then she is struck by the painful contrast between the children's mastery of their natural surroundings and their great discomfort and incompetence in the classroom. She summarizes the dilemma as "learning to sit still." Somehow, Matses children must suppress their spontaneous inclinations, which serve them well in learning their culture, and adopt a pattern of behavior and cognitive engagement that is completely novel. In the classroom they can't sit still, they can't remain silent. These children display the symptoms of what, in the context of a typical US classroom, would be labelled a "disorder."

Chaga peoples in rural Tanzania feel that schooling—especially too much reading and writing—is driving children "to the brink of hysteria." Moving north to the Sahara, Touareg boys aspire to sleep under the stars on a camel caravan. Touareg homes

> contain neither chairs nor tables ... people sit or lie on a mat, and constantly change their position ... sitting on a chair is the most unnatural thing in the world. And apart from the schoolchildren, no one stays inside a closed room [because] a closed room is like a prison.

In elementary schools in Denmark, Danish kids are "calm" while immigrants are "wild." Teachers use scolding and guilt to tame the wild ones. Historical examples of this mismatch between the proclivities of the child and the strictures of the classroom abound. From seventeenth-century Holland to eighteenth-century Japan, we can find a popular genre of painting that the Dutch called "unruly school scenes." What I want to suggest by these examples is that while evolution has shaped humans to be voracious learners—almost from birth—the conditions under which this learning takes place have almost never included anything that looks like contemporary classrooms, teaching, and lessons.

Morelli makes the point that Matses children are active learners, guided largely by their own curiosity and drive to master their environment. They enjoy enormous freedom to manage their own lives and are only gradually encouraged to bend to the demands of the family to do necessary chores. And, for most important skills that the child must learn, the hands-on approach works best. The rewards for the diligent learner are almost immediate—imagine the welcome a successful young fisher and his big catfish will enjoy.

As so many ethnographers before her, Morelli notes the conspicuous absence of "teaching" in the development of these children. Indeed, she believes that the Matses communities she studied—which had been transplanted from the deep forest interior to more accessible sites along major rivers—first learned to exploit new marine resources, such as these giant catfish, through their children. Boys, especially, being bold risk takers, were much quicker to adapt to the novel ecology than their parents. The parallel in contemporary society is quite obviously the use of computers—kids master them quickly and are tapped to help older, less facile, family members.

When queried about why they don't feel compelled to teach their children, parents provide a variety of explanations. Inuit "parents do not presume to teach their children what they can as easily learn on their own." On Pukapuka, in status-conscious Polynesia, to seek or receive instruction calls attention to one's inferior status. Aka "respect for an individual's autonomy is also a core cultural value . . . one does not impose his/her will, beliefs, or actions on others [including children]." Also quite common is the view that it is only when the child reaches a relatively mature and responsible state—in middle childhood—that they become really educable.

One may wonder about the relevance of observations of child rearing in small-scale traditional societies to today's educational challenges. But, as evolutionary psychologists have argued, the inherited suite of traits found in today's teachers and students did not evolve to allow better mastery of algebra. Those traits evolved in the context of making a living in a variety of natural environments. They evolved in a world where food was inevitably scarce and where children had to begin the process of learning self-sufficiency quite early. In the succeeding essays in this chapter, I'll try and trace the pathway from the pedagogy of the close-knit, self-sufficient village community to modern pedagogy in which—despite the blessings of sophisticated "instructional design"—it is still very hard to turn autonomous learners into diligent scholars.

The Roots of Schooling: Learning Must Be Paid For with Effort, Suffering, and Pain

In the previous essay, I characterized children as eager and enthusiastic learners of culture, but reluctant scholars. I would argue that the allegedly unsatisfactory performance of students and teachers may be better understood by a long view of the history of schooling. In this essay, I want to discuss two precursor institutions, as well as the earliest schools.

In many premodern societies, initiation rites may be the closest evident analogue to schooling. They are quite common cross-culturally and played a prominent role, even as small-scale societies became quite complex—the Inca, Spartans, and Aztec are good examples. These varied customs have actually been referred to as "bush schools." Like contemporary schools, initiation rites bring together same-age cohorts of youth in a specific place and period in their lives for "instruction" at the hands of adult experts. The "curriculum" and procedures are highly standardized and endure, largely unchanged, from generation to generation. However, the emphasis seems to be on indoctrination, not education or training. *Chisungu*, the lengthy girls' initiation in Bemba (Zimbabwe) society, includes "rites representing hoeing, sowing, cooking, gathering firewood ... but, instruction, in the European sense, was quite unnecessary in such subjects." By highlighting women's traditional occupations, the goal was not skill-training, as the girls were likely quite proficient already, but to affirm gender identity. A similar form of moralistic instruction may be found in male rites. Adolescents are perceived to need a degree of "repackaging" to reorient them from the peer group to the larger community, to reinforce their respect for authority, and to ready them for the responsibility of forming a family.

Because of their inherent mystery and secrecy, detailed descriptions of initiation rites are rare. However, a set of pedagogical principles can be extracted from cases in the ethnographic record. First, all initiation rites involve some element of body mutilation—ranging, mildly, from tattooing to scarification to the excision of the genitalia. The PNG Highlands and Sepik regions are particularly noted for the pain and utter terror associated with the process. Typically, the child is symbolically killed by a monstrous figure and then resurrected or reborn. In addition to painful injury, other anxiety-inducing treatments include forcible removal from one's home, confinement or seclusion in a strange place for an extended period, and physical ordeals such as bathing in ice water and running or dancing until exhausted. "The dominant theme of the initiation is that of an ordeal—trial and proof of maturity." Consequently, parents are spared from involvement in their child's initiation.

A second common theme is that the rites constitute an induction into the prevailing social order. For example, in the Bonerate circumcision ritual, "novices are formally introduced to the ideal standards of conduct to which adults should conform," including the appropriate display of shame and respect for others and acute awareness of their social position. Rites for girls emphasize subservience to senior women and obedience to one's future husband; and those for boys, subservience to senior men and dominance over women. The youth is forcibly weaned from the "bad influence" of the peer group or the mother. Didactic instruction in the "lore" of the society is not evident. On the contrary, the initiation rite is an opportunity to impress upon young people their ignorance and powerlessness. "In Kpelle society, secrecy ... supports the elders' political and economic control of the youth." Similarly, for Ngaanyatjarra aboriginal youth, sacred "knowledge had to be prized from [the elders] bit by bit, and with a lot of effort."

Another widely described institution found in small villages around the world, and continuing to expand in importance in the earliest states well through the Middle Ages, or, in places like Yemen, into the present, is the apprenticeship (the modern European model is quite different). In the apprenticeship, youth continue to learn through the same stepwise, observation/imitation procedure that characterizes their learning of nearly all aspects of their culture. There is very little explicit instruction by a master, and almost no verbal interchange. But an apprenticeship adds new elements. One such element is that parents are expected to pay a fee up front to induce the master to accept their child. In ancient Rome, a father wanting his son to learn the weaving trade would pay a fee *and* his son's room and board. The son is "bound" for a year, unable to leave his master for this minimum term.

In a typical apprenticeship, the master will probably *not* be the boy's father because a common ingredient is verbal and physical abuse of the apprentice by the master. Tukolor "fathers prefer that another weaver . . . train their sons . . . since they feel that they will not exert enough discipline in training." More generally, the hierarchical relationship between master and apprentice is of paramount importance. The master's knowledge is considered to have great worth, and the apprentice trades his or her labor and obeisance for access to that knowledge.

A steady diet of menial tasks in the earliest stage matches the apprentice's ability level, provides a kind of prepayment for the apprenticeship opportunity, and, most importantly, offers a measure—for the master to evaluate—of the apprentice's level of motivation. To become a potter in Japan, according to John Singleton, requires "a single-minded, wholehearted dedication to the craft . . . talent is to be developed through persistence, it is not considered . . . inherited or innate." In Tanon's thorough study of the Dioula (Ivory Coast) weaving apprenticeship, what is striking is the severe restriction imposed on what the apprentice can and cannot assay—compared to the relatively open access to and self-paced nature of learning opportunities in the village. The novice Dioula weaver is constrained to advance his skill in "baby steps," to reduce the likelihood of mistakes that an expert would need to rectify. Furthermore, the master takes advantage of the apprentice's free labor to assist with the more routine aspects of the master's own production. Like the initiation rite, the apprenticeship can seem like one long ordeal, and many apprentices sought to escape—a criminal offence.

Schooling has its origin in the apprenticeship. I make this claim largely on the basis of the many parallels between the character of the apprenticeship and the earliest schools. The first students, like apprentices, were drawn from a select group, because there were fees involved and specific prohibitions on students from the lower class or peasant communities. From school records, the earliest scribes were noted as the offspring of such luminaries as governors, senior civil servants, and priests. Corporal punishment was also essential to the conduct of schools—as it was to the apprenticeship.

The oldest known classroom and pedagogical material were found in Mesopotamia. The *edduba*, or Tablet House, from the third millennium BCE, excavated at Mari (in modern-day Syria), had two rows of benches for the students and many discarded tablets. The clay tablet facilitated instruction because it could be easily erased and reused and was much less costly than the writing media used elsewhere in antiquity. Kramer notes that the schools were "uninviting," the lessons were dull, and discipline was harsh. One poor novice describes his experience: "My headmaster read my tablet, said: 'There is something missing,' caned [to beat with a slender wooden rod or reed] me. 'Why didn't you speak Sumerian,' caned me. My teacher said: 'Your hand is unsatisfactory,' caned me. And so I began to hate the scribal art."

In Ancient Greece, "The teacher's badge of authority was the *narthex* ... the stalk of the giant fennel [which had] the capacity to hurt more than a hard stick." The Roman "schoolmaster's didactic tool of choice was the ruler or the whip: it enabled him to keep order amidst the rowdy crowd with which he was confronted on a daily basis." Even as schools evolved to more closely resemble contemporary practice, the teacher remained a remote and formidable authority figure, much like the master potter or blacksmith. In Britain, the "master" (teacher) is depicted perched at his elevated desk "grasping the birch—a bundle of twigs—that formed his badge of office" and used "to punish indiscipline and the inability to answer correctly." A teacher in Britain in the 1590s "laments that children are afraid to come to school and wish to leave as soon as possible because of the severity and frequency of the whippings." The teacher was therefore a daunting figure for children. These practices grew out of the belief that children would not naturally accept the role of student. An Egyptian proverb claimed that aspirant scribes had ears on their backs, implying that they must be beaten regularly or they won't listen.

Sumerian students, as young as seven, endured a many-year-long curriculum beginning with the menial tasks also characteristic of the apprenticeship. The students spent tedious hours every day copying over and memorizing long lists of names, technical terms, legal phrases, and whole dictionaries. Fragments of *ostraca*, or pottery shards, from Egypt show similar endless copying of prescribed texts. Students often were taught in a language that was not their mother tongue or even one they'd heard spoken. European schools employed Latin exclusively, so students learned to "recognize words and pronounce them, but they could not understand what they read." In thirteenth-century schools, "each student daily had to memorize a poem or story and recite it. When they did poorly they were beaten." Unlike the village "curriculum," the early school curriculum made little allowance for children learning through play, at their own pace, or through their own motivation and initiative. Autonomous learning is also thwarted because the school, like the initiation ritual, exercises complete control over access to knowledge. On the other hand, the payoff for the long-suffering student was quite evident: in the case of the initiation rite, it was formal acceptance as an adult or near-adult; for the apprenticeship and the apprenticeship-like schools, it was a secure income and elevated social standing for the rest of one's life.

It appears that, for the majority of its history, classroom instruction has provoked boredom and rebellion on the part of children. Controlling unruly students became the teacher's prime concern, and led to frequent corporal punishment, ostracism, and a very tense classroom atmosphere.

This is a pretty grim picture for sure. One gets the sense that it isn't just the children who chafe at the constraints of formal education. The societies themselves seem to approach these early schools with considerable reluctance—unlike, for example, the enormous enthusiasm invested in the raising up of warrior cohorts in so many societies, an enthusiasm shared by the young recruits. This suggests to me that the bedrock on which culture is based is not the patient transfer of knowledge from parents to children via carefully executed lessons, but, rather, the largely self-initiated, self-paced, and autonomous efforts of eager learners. Shortly, I'll discuss the parent as reluctant teacher, but in the next essay, I'll continue pursuing the roots of schooling up to the modern era.

Coercive Pedagogy: When "Education" Means Compliance

In the first essay in this chapter, "The Resistant Scholar," I described the eagerness and savvy that children apply to the enormous task of learning their culture, and contrasted that with a portrait of reluctant scholars rebelling against the strictures of the classroom and the curriculum. The scenario of children happily pitching in to assist, and learn their chores—using play in the early stages as an approximation and then taking baby steps through simple tasks within their grasp—is almost mythical. Nevertheless, it is a common denominator in virtually all of the hundreds of ethnographic accounts of childhood around the world. The contrast with the image of a sullen, rebellious "student" wearing a dunce cap in the corner of the classroom is striking.

But the village child-rearing system is not entirely hands-off. We can look at what happens when there's a gap between familial expectations for the child and their readiness and willingness to comply. One can compile a kind of "manual" of strategies that are widely employed to control children's behavior. In much of Asia and the Pacific, there are many occasions when children aren't permitted to behave like children. This might be during a public gathering or religious ceremony, or in the presence of non-family members. On Bali, children are expected to control their emotions at a young age; positive emotions, fear, and jealousy should all be hidden. Emotional restraint, modesty, and co-operation are also inculcated early on in young Chinese. These expectations are enforced through shame—claiming the child is making its mother unhappy, for example. Taiwanese mothers—with their errant child present—construct a narrative of current and past transgressions for an audience. They spotlight the child's misdeeds in front of others in order to provoke shame. Javanese cultivate the emotion of "*isin* ... (shame, shyness, embarrassment, guilt) so that at any formal public occasion children are exceedingly quiet and well-behaved and will sit docilely ... through hours and hours of formal speeches." On Fiji, the same emotions "are inculcated in the child by ridicule, mockery, laughter, or plain disapproval."

Ulithi islanders use ridicule to curb an errant child. Kaluli (PNG) mothers tease toddlers in order to discourage them from nursing, and children of any age are teased when they are greedy or disrespectful. From Borneo to the Native American Southwest, children are warned repeatedly that improper behavior can bring the wrath of some harmful being. Dusun (Borneo) parents regularly use fear of the supernatural as a means of ensuring that children conform to expected behavior. Parents tell children folktales with themes of violence inflicted on a child because of some error in his behavior. Among the Kaoka on Guadalcanal "the elders tell tales of the giants called *umou* that ... inhabit the remote mountains. These beings, they say, are ready to pounce on naughty boys and girls and carry them off to a cave, where the bodies are cooked and eaten."

Few realize that the utterly benign, Disney-fied fairy tales we are familiar with today are derived from much more potent sources. In the original Carlo Collodi version of Pinocchio—the tale that warns children of the perils of lying—Geppetto is accused of abusing the marionette/boy. After a stretch of imprisonment, Pinocchio returns to Geppetto's workshop where he kills the wise cricket. He is self-absorbed and has a penchant for making enemies, two of which, the fox and the cat, capture him and hang him from a tree.

If proverbs, shaming, teasing, and threats of the bogeyman aren't effective, many societies prescribe corporal punishment. The Matsigenka (Peru) punish the lazy or unco-operative by scalding or applying skin irritants. Freeman tallies the frequency and severity of child beating on Samoa, where they "believe in the unique efficacy of pain as a means of instruction ... severe discipline ... is visited on children from an early age." Corporal punishment is, thus, often seen as a legitimate tool in shaping the child's behavior. The Rwala Bedu (Syria) utilize an arsenal of physical punishments, ranging from spanking with a stick (small children) to smacking with a saber or dagger (older children). They hold that the rod of discipline leads to paradise. Mary Ainsworth recorded several episodes of physical punishment— for a variety of misdemeanors, including selfishness—in her observation in several Ganda (Uganda) villages.

Earlier in the chapter, I brought into the discussion the earliest instances of more formal, top-down instruction: namely the initiation rite, apprenticeship, and the first schools. The reader will recall that coercive tactics, particularly the assignment of onerous chores followed by physical and verbal abuse, are inherent in these institutions. And, of course, the initiation rite is almost entirely devoted to changing behavior through punishment.

Not surprisingly, we find that these tools from what I'm calling "coercive pedagogy" are still applied to children's schooling. In Asia, particularly, there is a long history of formal schooling with traditions of outstanding effort and achievement, which continues to the present. The cornerstone of this success is the relentless emotional socialization to develop powerful feelings of shame and guilt in the child that can be activated at any sign of slackened effort. The responsibility to push oneself to excel in school is fueled by the certainty that one's family, community, even one's ancestors', fate hangs in the balance. Corporal punishment may also be brought to bear on the reluctant scholar, particularly in China. Elsewhere, teasing, tongue-lashing, and physical punishment are widely employed by both parents and teachers to "motivate" reluctant scholars. And, dare I say, these methods are effective—at least to the extent of raising the level of student compliance and effort.

My point here is not that we should import our disciplinary tactics from another culture or turn the clock back to the "good old days" when teachers kept (and used) a paddle in the classroom (I was personally introduced to this method), but that an array of tactics to overcome children's academic malaise and resistance are now taboo. In postindustrial society, corporal punishment in school has largely been banned; legislators, courts, and child welfare agencies are widening the definition of "abuse" to include physical punishment by a parent of their own child. Teachers and parents are enjoined to protect the child's self-esteem and condemned for shaming the child by calling attention to his/her inadequate performance. As far as the bogeyman is concerned, he has been buried in a deep grave. Parents and teachers nowadays avoid *any* situation, however innocent, that might possibly frighten a child. Probably a majority of the world's different cultures incorporate costumed, masked figures whose public performance was often meant to frighten, especially the young. Today, even rubber, store-bought Halloween masks are too frightening to be admitted to the classroom.

Acceptable "inducement" strategies today include offering the child incentives (smiley faces) and attempting to "reason" with them. These "new" tactics to promote intellectual engagement and serious effort may be more socially acceptable, but less certain of success. Nevertheless, these ideas are being widely marketed. In

Sri Lanka, for example, a first-grade teacher said that "when she was a child, the teachers hit students for any kind of wrongdoing, even small children. But no longer. So what do they do with students who behave badly now? 'We must advise them,' she said." Ideally, the combination of engaging curriculum material, including textbooks and computer-based lessons, with a dynamic, creative, and supportive teacher should render coercion of any kind unnecessary. Unfortunately, whether one consults individual parents or the massive archive of education research, one finds this optimistic scenario to be rare and limited to a few, exclusive schools.

What I find ironic is that while we have, seemingly, removed coercive tactics from our pedagogy—whether at school or at home —we have replaced them with a tactic that, in its effects, is every bit as coercive. I'm referring to frequent, high-stakes academic testing. Now everyone has the opportunity to be chastised: parents, teachers, principals, school districts, and students, of course.

I also find it ironic that two opposing trends in US schooling policy have developed simultaneously. The first is the relentless expansion of testing to measure the student's precise level of achievement. The second is the growing tendency of schools to shield the individual student (and I include college students here) and his/her parents from any painful acknowledgment of the student's actual achievement.

Of Course "Good" Teaching Is Rare—Why Should We Expect Otherwise?

In spite of half a century or more of well-funded research, steadily growing school budgets, earlier and earlier onset of schooling, and heightened monitoring of teacher and student performance, indications of failure are legion—at least in the US. So far, in this chapter, I've reviewed some of the less well-known origins of this crisis. I pointed out that Matses boys would far rather "go fishing" than sit in a classroom listening to a teacher. I reviewed evidence to show that children—likely from the onset of the species—have taken the initiative in learning whatever is necessary. Very little of what they need to learn to survive can be articulated verbally or transmitted formally by a third party. Children learn virtually everything by doing it—through play when younger, and then through "doing chores" when older.

> The requirement of out-of-context, or context-independent, learning makes formal schooling an evolutionarily novel and "unnatural" experience ... *Children did not evolve to sit quietly at desks in age-segregated classrooms being instructed by unrelated and unfamiliar adults* [italics added]. Yet such procedures, to varying degrees, are necessary. They are necessary because the demands of modern culture required that children master basic technological skills, the most important of which are reading, writing, and mathematics, as well as knowledge in a broad realm of domains.

In *The Anthropology of Childhood*, I point out that the Reluctant Scholar also characterizes the behavior of many children in school today—perhaps the majority. College of Notre Dame students, interviewed by Susan Blum, claimed to "love" learning but "hate" school. Even students who claim to "love school" may, in fact, love socializing, playing on a team, performing in the school band or play—all primarily active, hands-on experiences. They may also declare that they love their teachers, but they willingly confess hatred of algebra ... and English ... and chemistry—learning experiences that tax the brain and not the body.

I see earlier institutions like the initiation rite, the apprenticeship, and the first scribal schools all contributing to the birth of mass schooling. Yet the "pedagogy" of such institutions clearly reveals an underlying assumption that, as soon as you introduce teachers, and a set, language-based (versus task-based) curriculum, you can also expect that students will resist. The atmosphere of these early schools and school-like institutions is one of students looking for any means to relieve the tedium, abuse, onerous work, and officious oversight of teachers. On the one hand, students "act up," and on the other, teachers punish. In the Renaissance as today: "The professional class included lawyers, notaries, governmental secretaries, university professors, physicians, and teachers in no clear order except for teachers at the bottom." Not a promising foundation.

It stands to reason that if children prefer to learn on their own initiative, and that this approach is successful—at least in adapting to premodern society—then parents may not see themselves as anything other than role models. Parents can also then be characterized as "reluctant"—at least as teachers. In the village, teaching is not only considered unnecessary, it may, in fact, be seen as counter-productive, as these statements show (all referenced in D. F. Lancy, *The Anthropology of Childhood: Cherubs, Chattel, Changelings*, 2nd edition (Cambridge: Cambridge University Press, 2015)):

- "Deciding what another person should do, no matter what his age, is outside the [Amazonian] Yequana vocabulary of behaviors. There is great interest in what everyone does, but no impulse to influence—let alone coerce—anyone. The child's will is his motive force."
- "'Equality' may be said to be the paramount value of the Asabano [PNG] and it is thus the mediating principle in interpersonal relations. Individuals both attempt to avoid infringing upon others, and are keen to ensure that their autonomy is not violated."
- "In a learning situation [in rural Tahiti] ... to tell anybody what to do ... is intrusive and taken as a sign of unjustified adult mood-driven irritability and impatience."
- "The relatively few restrictions placed on the young Okinawan child are an important basis for learning. By being able to participate freely, children learn what is going on in their village from day to day."

The contrast between these traditional views and our own is starkly illustrated in this comment by Alan Howard: "American

parents seem to feel that knowledge is something like medicine—
it's good for the child and must be crammed down his throat even
if he does not like it—Rotuman parents act as if learning were
inevitable because the child wants to learn."

In the previous essay, I showed that while children may be
eager learners, they aren't always eager workers. That is, on the
rare occasions when we see adults or older siblings intervening
in the otherwise largely autonomous behavior of children it is
usually to chastise them for sins of omission or commission.
That is, if we define teaching very broadly as attempting to
change the behavior of others, we see that reluctant teachers rely
almost entirely on various forms of coercion. This would include
subtle forms of correction, from using a pithy saying or proverb,
to gentle teasing, to scare tactics, to corporal punishment and
food denial. I'm not suggesting that "primitive" peoples enjoy
"abusing" their children. Rather, I'm arguing that, because
teaching is so rarely required in raising children, the traditional
pedagogical repertoire is quite limited. Carefully designed,
patient, child-centered lessons are very rarely reported in either
community or school contexts until quite recently.

The virtual absence of teaching in the ethnographic record has
not deterred a number of scholars from making very ambitious
claims re the universality of teaching, and it's likely that most
people would agree that it is the "parent's most important job."
But evidence to refute the notion that humans are all competent
teachers is, actually, much closer at hand. For example, I created
a simulation of a bedtime-story episode in the annex of an
elementary school in Phoenix. The room was set with a comfy
couch and a coffee table strewn with a sampling (from basic
"readers" to Caldecott winners) of age-appropriate books.
Working with the school, I selected a sample of thirty-two K-
1st-graders who ranged from extremely fluent to non-readers.
I invited a parent to come in to school and spend a half-hour
reading to their child—"as they would at home." I videotaped
these sessions. The results were as predicted: in sessions where
the parent (mostly the mother) effectively played a supportive

teaching role, the child displayed precocity as a reader, and vice versa. Parents who were clueless inadvertently placed obstacles in the path of their aspirant reader, who would, in all likelihood, struggle to become fully literate.

David Bjorklund carried out a very similar study with middle-class families, but the goal was to teach children to play chutes and ladders. Many parents were very good at this, carefully scaffolding the child's gradual learning. "Other parents were less supportive. Some provided no instruction, other than to correct children when they were wrong. Others did the computation for their children. Some insisted that children use a strategy that they were not capable of using." In another study, a sample of highly educated, middle-class American mothers displayed considerable variability in their effectiveness as teachers of their four-year-olds.

In conclusion, I would argue that disappointing school results arise, at least in part, due to two mistaken assumptions. First, that children's eagerness to learn and acquire mastery means they're somehow hardwired to assume the role of *student*. Failure to adequately fulfill this role is seen as a deviation from normal. On the contrary, children have escaped, avoided, or resisted the role of student/scholar. The second mistaken assumption is that parents are "born teachers," eager and willing to educate their children. Again, it is likely that parents are no more eager or confident to teach than are children to be taught. In trying to ensure an individual child's school success and, by extension, the success of all students, we are safer to assume that the roles of student and teacher must be assiduously cultivated. In the next essay, I will discuss specific parenting practices that are associated with children's early literacy and why they are not widely employed.

Talking like a Book

I want to reverse my usual direction of travel in this concluding essay of the chapter. Most of the suggestions in this book for raising children involve persuading mainstream parents that they could "lighten up" without doing irreparable harm to their offspring. These arguments have been buttressed by evidence from other cultures where laissez-faire is more the norm and kids turn out fine. But there is one area of parenting that does require close attention and intervention, and a laissez-faire stance is unhelpful. I'm referring to the need to shape children for the unfamiliar role of student and to prime the child with a suite of useful classroom skills. More specifically, I will focus on the parent's role in ensuring high levels of literacy—reading, writing, and speaking.

Anthropologist Shirley Brice Heath conducted a landmark study, published in the early 1980s, that highlighted the cultural basis of children's acquisition of literacy. In a poor, Southern, African-American community, referred to as "Tracton," use of books (other than the Bible) and printed material was limited, and parents did not engage in elaborate conversations with their young children, nor did they see it as their responsibility to act as the child's first teacher. She recorded sentiments that echo those recorded by anthropologists studying schooling throughout the world.

Heath also studied "Maintown," a community that was economically comfortable and where parents had considerable formal education. In contrast to Tracton, Maintown children's lives were saturated with literacy:

> as early as six months of age, children give attention to books and information derived from books. Their rooms contain bookcases and are decorated with murals, bedspreads, mobiles, and stuffed animals that represent characters found in books ... When children begin to verbalize about the contents of books, adults extend their question from simple requests for labels ... to ask about the attributes of these items ("What does the doggie say?" "What color is the ball?") ... Adults jump at openings their children give them for pursuing talk about books and reading.

Subsequent work by Catherine Snow and colleagues provided many additional cases of literary and nonliterary home environments. Scenes representing the latter condition included homes without any books, magazines, or newspapers, and parents who claimed never to read and who had no awareness of or involvement in the children's homework. Ms. Pagliucca "knew Derek went to the bookmobile . . . but she never asked to see his books or talked to him about what he was reading." Not surprisingly, the dominant family pastime was television viewing.

But mainstream parents don't stop at immersing kids in printed material and literary allusions. Another rich area of parental intervention is the "dinner-table" conversation. For very young children, these conversations promote the child's curiosity, its self-image as a learner of *things*, and its role as student vis-à-vis the parent-as-teacher. Creativity and cleverness are rewarded as well. "Mealtime [is] a richly supportive context for the use of rare words in informative contexts." Cross-national variation also appears as dinner-table "lessons" are somewhat different in middle-class French, Japanese-American, and Italian households.

Then we have parental intervention in children's make-believe play. Well-educated mothers encourage fantasy even before the child begins to pretend on its own. They do this by providing character toys and dolls and the props to go with them. Parents may model pretending for the child by holding up and making a stuffed animal or doll talk. With toddlers and preschoolers they provide play scripts and embellish their children's early fantasy constructions.

As Martini notes, "Children learn to 'talk like a book' before they learn to read." And it isn't just talk; children who enjoy a lengthy period of "emergent literacy" really are much more likely to learn to read before starting formal reading instruction, and more likely to enjoy reading. When quantitative comparisons are made, children exposed to greater amounts of narrative and explanatory talk were advantaged on a number "of language and literacy measures."

Referring back to my study of parent–child reading in the previous essay, I can add some further details. Mothers and their early readers displayed a degree of connoisseurship in sorting through the varied collection of picture books available. They paused to discuss those they were familiar with before selecting an inviting book they hadn't read. While they easily took turns reading aloud, there were digressions to admire the graphics or to comment on a funny or striking episode in the book. The child's enthusiasm remained high throughout and the parent was completely at ease.

In contrast, the mother–child pairs in which the child had been identified as "at risk" for reading failure were unable to engage as equals in the experience. Book selection was perfunctory, not an occasion for a mother–child discussion of children's books. Mothers tended to take the lead in selecting the books and they inevitably chose graded readers of the type used in school (but less frequently today). These books focus on word learning with only the barest attention paid to the characters or plot. They are, in a word, boring. Not surprisingly, the children read haltingly with many pauses. Their mothers stopped them to make corrections, even of their pronunciation. The experience was akin to a test as the child—urged on by the mother—struggles to correctly decode and pronounce individual words with no attention paid to story or characters. It was a painful experience for both.

Our interviews yielded responses that further widened this gap in terms of issues like regular bedtime stories, visits to the library, family members reading for pleasure, and elaborated parent–child discourse. These activities relate to literacy both directly and indirectly. For example, where children are exposed to the routine, order, and discipline inherent in a structured lifestyle, they are being socialized to play the role of student. The absence of these elements in children's socialization may well lead to the child becoming unco-operative, antisocial, and defiant. These traits, in turn, have been shown to interfere with the child's becoming literate.

Unfortunately, the number of children who experience a literacy-rich environment at home remains quite small. In much of the world, parents are ambivalent about their children's schooling. They may have other, more pressing priorities for them, including helping to care for their siblings, earning a living, or taking care of the herd. Even when village parents embrace schooling for their children, they don't command the suite of behaviors (reading stories, engaging in make-believe, dinner-table conversations) that introduce children to the literary practices associated with education and professional employment. Dinner-table conversations, bedtime stories, lingering visits to the library, and the like are also largely unavailable to children in poor and/or immigrant communities in countries with a developed, modern economy. These practices for enhancing literacy are embedded in one's culture, transmitted informally from one generation to the next.

Absent a rich emergent literacy experience, children don't seem to "catch up" once they're in elementary school. At least that's one conclusion we might draw from surveys indicating that only about 50 percent of students *who elect to enroll in college* or other tertiary schooling are actually able to read sufficiently well to succeed in more advanced studies. Even more alarming are the results from a very thorough survey which found a significant, recent *decline* in reading by younger Americans. Recreational reading, especially by teenagers, has rapidly declined, in step with the increase in Internet use. In a 2002 survey, less than one-third of thirteen-year-olds read daily. A very recent survey found that 45 percent of US seventeen-year-olds admit to rarely, if ever, reading for pleasure. As voluntary reading has plummeted, literacy rates have also declined. Replicating and extending the emergent literacy practices of well-educated parents—as recommended by the experts—appears to be an enormous challenge.

I very much fear that we are not only failing to spread the gospel regarding early-childhood home literacy activities, but we may be losing ground. One could make a very good case that extracurricular activities, electronic media, and harried parents conspire to reduce, if not curtail, parent–child literacy sessions, including joint storybook reading. The effects may be more easily detected from studies of children's voluntary reading than from standardized test scores. There are READERS, and there are readers.

7   The Consequences of Raising "Unique Individuals"

As I discussed in Chapter 1, most children grow up in a gerontocracy where they have very low status. This dictates their relationships vis-à-vis those older than themselves. A Fijian child, as young as four, is expected to bow very low and avoid eye contact when passing an adult, and may be cuffed for failing to show sufficient respect. On Java, there are similar strictures, as well as the requirement to use proper, polite speech when addressing one's older relatives. In more egalitarian societies, there is often a great emphasis on sharing and avoiding any display of selfishness. A Kaoka "toddler presented with a piece of fruit is told to give half to 'So-and-so,' and should the order be resisted, the adult ignores all protests and breaks a piece off to hand to the child's companion."

A common theme of many folktales—often aimed didactically at children—is the eventual comeuppance of a disobedient, self-centered child. As the Japanese proverb says, "The nail that sticks out gets hammered down." The ideal is that children are to rapidly adapt to their assigned niche in the family and community. They are encouraged and rewarded for their politeness and helpfulness, but chastised for making demands (nursing infants the exception), interrupting an adult conversation, or being underfoot. They eat the food allotted to them from the family meal. If they balk at the menu, they'll go hungry. Criticism and punishment are far more common than praise and reward. Fitting in usually means being placed under the supervision of an older sibling or grandmother since one's parents are busy working or caring for an infant. If all this sounds primitive and harsh, consider that it would have been the norm until at least the middle of the last century. And it still prevails among many conservative communities such as Orthodox Jews or the Amish, as well as in first- and second-generation immigrant families—especially from Asia. A common refrain during my own youth was, "Children should be seen and not heard."

Oh, how we've changed! Consider the central message of the animated film *Zootopia*. Judy Hopps, the main character, spurns the admonitions of her family and rural community to continue their traditions and become a carrot farmer. Instead, she becomes—after flagrant insubordination—the first bunny cop in the city of Zootopia.

Heidi Keller has developed a compelling explanation of these contrasting expectations for children and their parents:

> Euro-American or German middle-class mothers . . . focus on children's agency and mental states, preferences, wishes, and needs, whereas mothers with an interdependent cultural model of parenting, such as Chinese or rural Nso mothers, focus on the social context, moral obligations, and respect. These differences are already prevalent in interactions with babies that are only a few months old.

Contemporary Euro-American, middle-class culture emphasizes the child's becoming a highly unique individual who is not obligated to conform to cultural patterns of long standing. I seem to recall a steady diet of Raisin Bran as a child. It was THE family breakfast food. Today, one can find a different cereal in the pantry for each member of the family—chosen particularly by the young consumers, with little consideration for nutritional value or the tastes of other family members. Again, fifty years ago it was customary, among all but the very rich, for clothes to be passed down from sibling to sibling (or cousins). This would be unthinkable today, even though "distressed" jeans make a fashion statement. (It's actually far worse, as children reject generic labels and clearance racks in favor of designer labels and full retail prices.) The child is, in most situations, accorded the same status as an adult. This plays out most dramatically when a child interrupts a conversation between two adults and the adult addressed breaks off the conversation to attend to the child, leaving his/her conversational partner "on hold."

Once the individualization genie is let out of the bottle, it is nearly impossible to get it back in again. Anthropologists and sociolinguists have undertaken numerous observational studies of mealtime in middle-class households. Here's an all-too-typical scene:

SHANTA: Tuna or salmon?
VIRAT: No, no.
SHANTA: NO, you cannot have-uh-that. [Jello]
VIRAT: No, no, no, no, no! (whining) I want some Jello.
SHANTA: You cannot have Jello.
VIRAT: Yes I can.

Like many of our parents, Shanta attributes to her young child, five-year-old Virat, the competence to make desirable health-conscious decisions. By asking an open-ended question about what the child wants to eat, Shanta sets the stage for bargaining and invites Virat to choose his own option, ostensibly from the entire contents of the fridge and freezer. Yet Shanta already has particular foods in mind—tuna or salmon. Despite this, she proceeds to argue with him when he offers an unacceptable choice.

To those who would like their family to avoid this fate, let me recommend the Munchkin Baby Food Grinder (and other brands) available at Amazon for $7.50. Our children's first "meals," aside from nursing, consisted of mashed portions of the food we were eating—at the *family* dinner table (our younger daughter in a "hook-on" high chair). There are other situations where children may benefit from the opportunity to make choices (the library), but should these include diet and important family activities?

In fact, the entire custom of family mealtimes is under siege. In the US, a family member shares, on average, fewer than five meals per week with other family members. This has happened for at least three reasons. First, almost daily extracurricular activities,

Figure 7.1. Ballerina

such as organized sports (where parents act as chauffeur, coach, and cheerleader) and homework, fall into the time slot historically set aside for preparing and eating dinner. From a long-term study of middle-class US families, this is a typical parenting schedule:

> Most of the children had to be driven to extracurricular activities several afternoons a week. They also needed help completing homework assignments due the following day. Children needed a "parent–manager" who kept tabs on where they had to be, when they had to be there, what they needed to bring with them, what homework assignment to prioritize, and how to pace one's progress on a long-term school project. In addition, parents needed to make sure that their kids got a snack to keep them going, did their homework correctly, and performed to the best of their abilities during their extracurricular activities.

It is very hard to discover a niche in this stream of activities that could be devoted to the "family dinner hour." But a second, less obvious reason for the disappearance of the family dinner is that food marketers have responded profitably to the individualization trend.

> While parents valued the "Family Dinner" ritual, they found it difficult to achieve ... the decline of the family dinner [is due in part to] the enormous consumption and use of single-serving, pre-prepared "convenience" foods ... the ubiquity of microwaveable, individual-sized, packaged snacks in the home undermined children's interest in even coming to the dinner table, much less their willingness to eat what had been prepared for them.

Last, but not least, we don't need systematic research to assure us that social media, an all-absorbing *individual* activity, has eroded, if not obliterated, many customary occasions for social intercourse. At any restaurant, it is easy to find tables where all the diners are engaged with their own smartphone or tablet, rather than each other.

The gradual disappearance of the family gathering for dinner is more significant than a simple "lifestyle change." Children who eat dinner with their parents five or more days a week have less trouble with drugs and alcohol, eat more healthily, show better academic performance, and report being closer with their parents than children who eat dinner with their parents less often. Studies done in the not-too-distant past identified the "family dinner" ritual as linked to academic success, primarily through children's enhanced narrative fluency and general literacy. There are many "academic" components in the typical family dinner conversation.

> Parents engage children in teaching routines. Typically, a child asks "Why?" and the parent answers at length. Common topics are aspects of the physical world: sea life, animals, dinosaurs, stars, astronauts, and how everyday things work ... parents and children invent stories, jokes, and riddles. They set up "what if"

scenarios and experiment with new ways of doing things. Parents listen to, watch and comment . . . Children learn to "show off" . . . inventing songs, jokes, games or implausible situations . . . parents also laugh when children break rules or violate expectations in imaginative ways.

In 1955, "well-brought-up" children demonstrated an early awareness of social conventions, such as using polite speech around adults and addressing them by title/last name—never by their first name. And an attitude of appreciation toward one's parents, teachers, and others to whom one is indebted was expected. Adults felt licensed to chastise and correct politeness lapses or misbehavior in other people's children. Today, the absence of these positive attributes in their children provokes indifference or puzzled anguish on the part of parents. What is most striking to me about the sea change in child rearing that has occurred during the last fifty years is that *nothing else has changed.* We live in the same sorts of neighborhoods, attend the same churches, take the same family vacations, drive the same cars, and sit for hours in the same classrooms. Television programs are still pretty bad, only in different ways. We have better tools, but we still do much the same jobs (how different is computer programming from accounting?) as sales clerks, managers, automobile assemblers, and stage actors.

In other words, the great shift in child-rearing philosophy did not occur as a necessary adaptation to a changed culture. There have been no game-changing breakthroughs in medicine, for example, that dictated this shift. Just the opposite has occurred: the spontaneous change in how we view and raise our children is affecting the broader culture. In 1955, children were not yet a marketing demographic; now they are one of the most important. In 1983, $100 million was spent on marketing to children. Twenty years later, that figure had grown to $17 billion.

In the essays that follow, I want to continue this analysis and diagnosis of some of the central tenets of the "new" approach to childhood, where uniqueness is valued above all social conventions.

What's in a Name?

In a typical semester, I may have in my class Holli, Aleece, Katelyn, Janaea, Kerington, Raiven, Mace, Kierra, Jera, and Kamron. Roughly 10–20 percent of the class has been given a unique name not found in the Bible, not shared with a venerated kinsman, and not listed in *Who's Who*. Actually, these are comparatively tame examples. The roster of names from our football squad is even more marquee-minded. From experience, I know that trying to spell these names will be difficult for the myriad teachers, clerks, and record keepers of all stripes who'll often get it wrong, with unfortunate consequences for the nominally challenged. Pronouncing them is by no means a walk in the park, either. That's because a straightforward phonetic rendering of the written name isn't always reliable. Ki-er-a is Ker-a, Al-ee-s is Al-is, Jan-A-ah is Jan-a and so on. On the other hand, we find common names with unorthodox spellings. *Qathrin* or *Paeslee* hint that the parents may be only semiliterate and can't spell. The latest trend, according to colleague and mother of two Jennifer Delliskave, is to toss a few numbers into the name, as in Cat3ine, Four-Oh-Seven, Jupe6, Cruzin4U, ANUT4U, and Trouble101. What were they thinking of? Vanity license plates? Future Rapper? Droid? Ham radio operator? Gang banger? Giving them a strong but memorable password? I expect to see a spike in "Brexit." There was a time when unusual names were favored only by rock and movie stars (Dweezil, Moon Unit, Elijah Blue) who could afford to erect an antibullying shield around their oddly named offspring. No longer.

One wonders why parents would inflict a novel name on a child, given the likely consequences. I have an answer, but I'll beg the reader's patience as I tell the larger story first.

In my survey of the tremendously varied body of reports on children by anthropologists, interesting naming conventions can readily be found. Many such conventions are based on a view of children very different from our own. Infant mortality from illness, malnutrition, and infanticide has meant that infants are not treated as fully human. Aside from essential care, they may be largely ignored. The Ayoreo explain that should the child die, the loss will not be so deeply felt. Aka infants are not considered to be complete humans, and in fact are thought to be wandering in a very vulnerable existence somewhere between life and death. Aka do not name a child for as long as half a year after birth. A Roman child wasn't accepted as a member of the family for eight to nine days after birth, when, in the *lustratio* rite, it was named. Infants may be seen as having one foot in the spirit world and one in the material. Hence the conferral of personhood—including a "real" name—is often delayed.

For the Beng people of Côte d'Ivoire, naming reflects the belief that babies are ancestors who've been reincarnated and returned from *wrugbe*, the land of the dead. Consequently, Beng adults not only treat infants with great respect and devotion, but talk to them as well, believing the child/ancestor can serve as an intermediary with powerful spirit forces. This conception of children also works to cushion the shock of infant death. In Indonesia, the Balinese hold similar beliefs. Spirits of ancestors return to inhabit the infant in the womb. Following birth, the baby is believed to be divine for a period of 210 days. This *recycling* of persons who've passed on is quite common, also practiced by the Inuit, for example. Among the Yoruba, children "are watched for the unfolding of resemblances to the ancestors they reincarnate." Note that there is no expectation that the child is born with its own, unique "self." Rather, the child is invested with someone else's name, as well as their identity.

Recycling of an identity via naming can take many forms. In India, the firstborn male is named after the paternal grandfather, the second after the distaff counterpart, and so on back through the family tree. The same thing was true in nineteenth-century England. European royalty have always recycled names (think Henry VIII) and, among the working class, a generic name like Smithson (son of a blacksmith) was typical. In early America, *necronyms* were common. A newborn son was often named after an earlier-born male who'd died. Hence one finds two or even three Robert Evanses inscribed on family headstones, as infant mortality claimed one-third of all children. Not surprisingly, the total stock of names remained small.

It seems paradoxical, but names may project a profound anonymity rather than a unique identity. Yoruba infant names include *Abidemi*—translated as *boy or girl born whilst his/her father is out of town*; *Ajayi*—*A boy born with his head facing downwards,* and *Ige*—*A boy or girl born feet first* (breech). On Bali, every firstborn male is named *Wayan*, *Made* for the second-born, and so on. Imagine being in a classroom where one-fourth of the male students had the same name? Those poor teachers.

Anonymity can be conveyed in a less benign manner. For the Korowa of Papua New Guinea, *Famine, Hungry,* and *Wanting Sago* are popular children's names, reflecting the fact that a child is in a state of pronounced want, dependent on others for its well-being. Among the Yomut of Turkmenistan, when a girl is born, it is common practice to give her a name expressing the wish for a son. Girls' names such as *Boy Needed* (*Oghul Gerek*) or *Last Daughter* (*Songi Qiz*) are common.

Anonymity for Puritan children was an inevitable result of the practice of using one's children as human sandwich boards, marketing the parents' beliefs. A sampling of names applicable for boys or girls: *Abstinence, Diffidence, Tribulation, Sorry-for-sin,* and *Hate-evil. Flee-fornication* was a name given to illegitimate children to remind them not to fall into the same sin their parents had. This practice lives on as contemporary parents with a religious bent can send little Messiahs out into the world (762 Messiahs were issued US Social Security cards in 2012). Someone dug up this fact in connection with a celebrated legal case in which a judge refused to permit Jaleesa (*sic*) Martin to name her little missionary "Messiah." The decision was later over-returned because the judge's rationale that "there was only one Messiah" violated the Establishment Clause of the United States Constitution.

Sometimes the use of names to obscure the child's identity (rather than enhance it) can be for the child's protection. The

Fulani (West Africa), for example, roll a child in dung or give it a name such as *Birigi* (cow turd) to make it less attractive and immune to malicious jealousy. Among the Macha Galla of Ethiopia, one precaution against malevolent jealousy—common throughout the ethnographic record—includes the Galla use of "bad" names, usually those of the Mao or Nuak, the indigenous ethnic groups from whom the Galla took slaves.

Contemporary naming customs, in contrast, are designed to ensure that the child will "be somebody" from birth, a unique individual—just the opposite of the nonpersonhood and anonymity that has been characteristic of childhood for millennia. A typical rationale for unique names that I've heard includes: "We love the name Amy, but Amy's too common. We want our daughter to stand out in a crowd. We want her to be different. That's why we're naming her Amie." This search for unique names can be carried to extremes as, for example, the case of a Swedish couple who gave their child the genderless appellation "Pop." Their explanation: "We want Pop to grow up more freely and avoid being forced into a specific gender mold from the outset; it's cruel to bring a child into the world with a blue or pink stamp on their forehead." A very recent manifestation of the uniqueness craze is for children as young as three to spend hours daily making their own (or watching others') YouTube videos of routine events in their lives. They aren't just "experiencing childhood, but constantly considering how their experiences will be perceived by an audience."

Pasting a designer, rather than generic, label on one's newborn is part of a larger phenomenon in which parents commit to the notion that each child is unique, and that this distinctiveness should be nurtured and facilitated. This contrasts sharply with the far more common practice of socializing children to "fit in," which includes being respectful and considerate of others, acting responsibly, and helping out by doing chores. In contrast, parents of *haut couture* individualists specifically reject this view, as revealed in a vignette recorded by Gross-Loh:

> Molly, a seven-year-old, suddenly declared to her friend Lila, "I'm tired of playing with you today." Later Lila's mother brought it up with Molly's mother, Eve, who told her that Molly was "just being honest." Eve saw nothing wrong with Molly's hurtful words; after all, she was raising her daughter to know that it was important to recognize and express her own feelings.

One offshoot of the trend for "raising unique individuals" is the search for the child's "passion." Lisa Heffernan has written a thorough critique of this movement which, apparently, has been triggered by changes in the admissions criteria of elite colleges. No amount of time and money must be spared in the search for the child's passion, which, once found, now serves as the justification for the entire family to worship and pay homage to the impassioned child. The flip side of raising unique, very special children is raising "nice" children. A Harvard psychologist has developed a menu of strategies to ensure that children are raised to be sensitive, caring, and polite. When older children are interviewed about this dichotomy, they acknowledge that parents convey the message that the child's academic performance and/or their happiness is far more important than their considerate treatment of others. So, in the vignette above, we might say that Eve should be encouraging Molly to show concern for the feelings of others rather than to "recognize and express her own feelings."

"Being special" doesn't stop at age seven or eight, but extends into adulthood. When the individual is charting her own course she is given a pass in terms of complying with social norms. My favorite story that links unique naming with freedom from social constraints is the long-running Bristol Palin saga.

The saga begins in 2012 when Bristol's mother Sarah—against all odds—is selected as John McCain's running mate as the candidate for vice president of the United States. Aside from Bristol, Sarah was clearly committed to establishing the uniqueness of her offspring via original names, e.g. Willow (female), Trigg (male), Piper (female) and Track (male). Continuing that tradition, Bristol's two children are named Tripp (male) and Sailor (female). In case anyone might have forgotten, Sarah Palin's main asset as a candidate was her moral righteousness. Certainly her service as Alaska's governor was undistinguished, except in its abrupt end when she quit eighteen months before her term ended. Palin's moral credentials were bolstered by her daughter Bristol becoming a paid (six figures in 2009) spokesperson for the "abstinence-before-marriage" movement. No one in that movement or in Sarah Palin's constituency seemed at all troubled by the fact that Bristol had, a year earlier, given birth to a bastard. In most tribal societies, and Western society until recently, she would have been ostracized, hidden away from society, or banished to live with some distant relative—but not in this century. Bristol is praised for not having an abortion. She repeated this feat at the end of 2015, giving Sailor an illegitimate brother, Tripp. Nevertheless, since she's so "special," she was able to continue as a paid spokesperson for the "abstinence-before-marriage" movement. She has become a well-paid media personality who has successfully capitalized on her "lapses," including a tell-all account of losing her virginity in her 2011 memoir.

Aside from anecdotes which any of us can conjure at a moment's notice, a very important and thorough survey of decades of empirical work on national character concludes, "Americans are the most individualistic people in the world."

Another way to think about this phenomenon appears when you consider the "tiger mom" model. In that (mainly East Asian) view, there is one, and only one, path to success. The tiger mom's job as parent is to persuade, cajole, and punish her child to stay on that path and, above all, get ahead of others. In the West, the opposite view holds that each child should follow their own path. There are at least two problems with that approach. First, it is impractical because there are far more individual pathways that lead to failure in life than to success—100,000 people in prison for every Bill Gates. Second, many, if not most, children following a unique path will encounter serious obstacles which turn their parents into helicopters and snowplows, hovering anxiously, then swooping down to clear the obstacles.

Returning to child-naming fashions, one might ask if there are consequences for those who have rare or invented names. In fact, there are. In research dating back to a study at Harvard in 1948, researchers have consistently found that having a rare name acted as a handicap. This is mainly because others—teachers, peers, employers—tend to undervalue or feel prejudice against those with rare names. This research suggests that one's name may influence one's choice of profession, school admission and performance, whom to marry, and the likelihood of not being hired over others with more conventional names.

For my part, I'm sending a donation to the Institute for Naming Children Humanely, a nonprofit organization dedicated to achieving a better society through better names for children.

Trash Talking or Taking Out the Trash

When I read the newspaper, my attention is sometimes riveted by items that others might overlook. For example, I was drawn to a news item where a ten-year-old boy stabbed his mother in the back following an argument about doing chores. While checking to see if this might just be an isolated case, Google led me to several other child-on-parent attacks following a chore request. These include Deborah L. McVay of Canton, Ohio, shot dead by her son following a disagreement over chores. A case in California involved a fourteen-year-old killing both parents following an argument over taking out the trash. It turns out these cases may lie at the tip of an iceberg.

There has been a steady stream of articles published recently by social scientists reporting on children and chores or, more formally, on the development of social responsibility. One study that has received a great deal of attention was carried out over several years at UCLA and involved hundreds of hours of close observation of family life. The researchers report, "Comparative analysis reveals that most children in our study spend surprisingly little time helping around the house ... children's participation in household work is minimal."

Across 30 families observed, no child routinely assumed
responsibility for household tasks without being asked. Children
were assigned tasks and intermittently made their bed, or cleared
the table, or got dressed on their own. But the overall picture was
one of [fruitless] appeals by parents for help with practical
matters, relying on politeness markers such as, "please," offers of
rewards, or veiled threats. Parents also frequently directed a child
to help them and then backtracked and did the task themselves . . .
[Otherwise] children resisted or flatly refused.

This study has been replicated in middle-class suburbs in Australia
and several European countries. For example, in West Berlin, "The
parents alone are responsible for the reproduction of daily life . . .
The child is the *recipient* of care and services." When the rare chore
is assigned, children expect to be paid for it. Further examples
follow (D. F. Lancy, *The Anthropology of Childhood: Cherubs,
Chattel, Changelings*, 2nd edition (Cambridge: Cambridge University Press, 2015)):

- In a case study from Los Angeles, a parent spends a lot of time
  cajoling/guiding a five-year-old into making her bed. It
  becomes a big dramatic production after she initially refuses,
  claiming incompetence. In a comparative case from Rome, the
  father doesn't even bother trying to get his eight-year-old
  daughter to make her bed, he does it himself, while complaining that her large collection of stuffed animals and her decision
  to move to the top bunk make his task much harder.
- "[Genevan children] use the vociferous defeat strategy. They
  comply with what is asked of them but . . . cry, scream, bang
  doors, lock themselves up in their rooms to sulk and so on . . .
  Some . . . agree to submit if their parents can prove their
  demands are well-founded. [They may resort to an exchange]
  'I do a chore at home and she lets me go out . . .' Some count on
  the strategy of *fait accompli* . . . they do what they want without
  asking for permission, even if this means they will be reprimanded later. One boy mentioned employing a kind of 'terrorism.' That is, he attacks his parents when they refuse something:

'I shout at them, that they are rotten, not nice, that they have no heart, I sulk, I become bad, I pester them and sometimes I hit them a little.'"

- A lengthy description of "shepherding" a four-year-old [Swedish] child to bed at night shows this as a major undertaking [consuming] the mother's time and energy.

Well, what can anthropology teach us? The gap between childhood in premodern and contemporary society is nowhere wider than on this issue. Universally, children are expected to volunteer to help out and they respond eagerly. Indeed, so eager are they to fit in and be useful, they sometimes need to be directed away from tasks that are dangerous or beyond their capacity.

The small child shown in Figure 7.2, whose name is Katerina, was the subject of a film documenting her life and that of her

Figure 7.2. Katerina

family. The filmmaker, Ivan Golovnev, follows Katerina from two to four and a half years of age. She lives with her parents and older brother in northwestern Siberia. The family—belonging to the seminomadic Khanty tribe—forage, fish, and herd reindeer. In their camp and the vicinity there is no evidence of a school, a church, government building (or any permanent structure), electricity, running water, or (*sacre bleu!*) television. From the first, as a wobbly toddler, Katerina is shown being helpful. She carries firewood chopped by her mother into their tent, ladles food from a large pot over the fire into a tin (which she can barely manage to carry), and feeds the dog. She carries a pan with bread dough to her mother to place in the baking oven. When her mother goes gathering in the forest, Katerina has her own toddler-size collecting bucket. She is out in all weather, including deep snow—keeping warm in her animal-skin anorak. She's completely at ease in close company with large shepherd dogs and reindeer. A further sampling of folk wisdom on this subject from the ethnographic record follows (all referenced in D. F. Lancy, *The Anthropology of Childhood: Cherubs, Chattel, Changelings*, 2nd edition (Cambridge: Cambridge University Press, 2015)):

- "Remember that in the Beng language, one word for 'child' really means 'little slave.' As soon as the little one can walk confidently, don't hesitate to send your child on errands in your village or neighborhood."
- "Every small [Ghanaian Talensi] boy of six–seven years and upwards has a passionate desire to own a hen."
- Make-believe play was particularly low in Nyansongo (Kenya) probably because children there participated early in real adult work and therefore did not need to "practice" through acting out.
- "In accord with the belief that lactation uses up maternally irreplaceable body substances, it is seen [in rural Mexico] as incurring debts on the part of children, who thus are obligated to attend their mother's wants."

- "Initial efforts at subsistence work are recognized by giving them food, and by calling other people's attention to a child's effort ... [Murik—PNG] mothers [thus] encourage a strong association between work, recognition, and being fed."
- "Only when the [Sudanese] Nuer boy tethers the cattle and herds the goats ... cleans the byres and spreads the dung to dry and collects it and carries it to the fires is he considered a person."
- "This assumption of work and responsibility comes about gradually, and largely on the Chiga [Uganda] child's own initiative."

Surveying the hundreds of cases recorded by anthropologists, we find, among the commonest chores, children, particularly girls, helping care for infants and assuming full-time care of toddlers; younger children running errands and helping others in various household activities; boys herding livestock from an early age; children of both sexes working in gardens; young foragers proudly bringing home gathered foods and small game. Typically, chores are prime opportunities for learning. The young hunter's or fisher's careful observation of those who are more competent, coupled with many trials, gradually leads to mastery and a larger catch. A girl may start out weaving on a "toy" loom—which still produces useable fabric—and gradually improves speed and technique until she produces textiles of a size and quality rivaling those of her older female kin. In middle childhood (ages seven to ten) children's chores become their jobs. That is, they have a set of tasks that they are responsible for and they no longer have to be told or asked to carry out these tasks. They are now considered competent, responsible, and reliable. Historians tell similar tales. In colonial America, children were to display "reverent courtesy" to their parents at all times. How could they submit to the will of God if they didn't first submit to their parents' will? Girls of four knit stockings and mittens; at six they could spin flax and comb wool. Boys took care of animals, chopped firewood, picked berries, etc.

Children, however, are no longer held responsible for household chores and the care of siblings, while parents despair at raising parasites that have little sense of responsibility. This essay would become much too long were we to trace the history of this dramatic change. Excellent sources are available for those who're interested. I believe that many contemporary parents would argue that they really want to instill a sense of responsibility in their children and do include "doing chores" in their parenting model. But they would also report considerable frustration at their children's resistance. I distinctly recall a news item relating how a suburban couple in Florida, the Barnards, had gone on strike and moved into a tent in their driveway, refusing to cook, clean, or otherwise care for their teenage children until they agreed to mend their ways and help out with household chores. Earlier they had tried awarding smiley faces and withholding allowances, to no avail.

I think the disconnect between our expectations for our children and their actual behavior arises due to a few critical changes in child-rearing philosophy. First, as discussed in the introduction to this chapter, we are now raising *individuals*. By raising unique individuals, we grant children unprecedented authority to "decide" for themselves. As we've seen, they may decide not to carry their dishes to the dishwasher, or decide not to tidy up their room or put the cap back on the toothpaste. Because we are raising them to focus on their own needs, preferences, and wishes, they aren't focused on the needs, preferences, and wishes of others, especially other family members. Second, parents are super-busy and take advantage of an array of child-unfriendly appliances and other aids, reducing opportunities to engage children in routine household chores. Wouldn't it be nice if our otherwise unengaged four-year-olds could drive us to and from work? In the village, there are dozens of tasks which children can undertake successfully and safely—not the case in modern suburbia.

Third, I've found this striking anomaly in children's development. From the anthropological literature, it is abundantly clear that even very young children are at a fever pitch to get involved and be helpful to others. In a psychology experiment done some years ago, the investigators found that children as young as eighteen months "spontaneously and promptly assisted the adults in a majority of the tasks they performed. Furthermore, the children accompanied their assistance by relevant verbalizations and by evidence that they knew the goals of the tasks, even adding appropriate behaviors not modeled by the adults." This finding has been replicated and considerably broadened. Eighteen-month-old children assist without being asked and without even making eye contact with the person needing help. In another study, children overcame obstacles placed in their path in order to assist, and could not be seduced by a play opportunity from trying to assist. Evidently, "young children have an intrinsic motivation to act altruistically."

I believe that this striving to be helpful, if unrewarded by the assignment of chores, is extinguished. Children, eventually, stop volunteering. Instead, they get a free ride and when, finally, at eight or later, chores are assigned, the window of opportunity is closed. They've been conditioned to receive care, not give it. They no longer worry about fitting in or engaging in reciprocal relations with caretakers. They can, correctly, assume that lavish care will be available no matter how little effort they put into supporting parents and the household. They refuse to do chores, or, worse, hurl invective, slam doors, and withdraw from active membership in the family circle.

This failure to involve each child in family and household support activities may have other, unfortunate effects. In Marty Rossmann's research, she found that assigning chores, or encouraging helping, generally instilled in children the importance of contributing to their families and gave them a sense of empathy as adults. Those who had done chores as young children were more likely to be well adjusted, have better relationships with friends and family, and be more successful in their careers.

The solution must be twofold. Above all we must recognize that our "passion" to raise unique, "special," and perfect children may have unintended consequences of the sort we've just been discussing. Hierarchy, consideration of others, acquiescence to decisions made on one's behalf by parents, and shyness in expressing wishes, likes, and dislikes may actually be necessary to the healthy development of children. More narrowly, parents need to take time to find chores for three- and four-years-olds, recognizing that their "help" may actually mean more work for the parent. I am always heartened in the supermarket when I see a youngster pushing a child-sized grocery cart filled with items. Perhaps the parent is pushing a larger cart to handle the overflow. Perhaps the child's cleaning of the bathtub leaves a ring the parent would have removed. Perhaps the child mixes up the socks when putting away the laundry. OK, so, perhaps the "made" bed still has a few wrinkles in the bedspread. Perhaps the family relies on plastic dinner plates until the kitchen helper gets a little less clumsy. Might parents "market" their child to friends as a "babysitter?" It's obviously harder for us to create appropriate and meaningful chores than for a family with a barnyard full of animals and a garden full of weeds, but it can be done.

Failure to Launch

The term "failure to launch" is an increasingly popular way to describe the difficulties many youth face when transitioning into the adolescent and adult phases of development which, progressively, demand greater striving, self-sufficiency, and responsibility. The phenomenon is, in fact, so commonplace that it has attracted many social satirists. Hollywood got in on the act with *Failure to Launch*, a 2006 romantic comedy. In the movie, "Tripp," a thirty-five-year-old man, lives in the home of his parents and shows no interest in leaving the comfortable life his parents, especially his mother, have made for him there. His mother cooks his breakfast, washes his laundry, and vacuums his room. He is "rescued" by a young woman who falls in love with him and is determined to transfer Tripp's dependency from his parents to her.

I want to do two things in this essay. First, I will try and address the question whether, as anthropologists, we see the failure-to-launch syndrome in our studies, and what it looks like. Next I will try and elucidate the origins of the syndrome in our culture.

Rockets and large ships are "launched," closely akin to a plane's "taking off." All three cases involve prior periods of construction and preparation. A ship needs a slipway, a rocket needs a launch pad, and a plane requires a runway. Electronics and communications must be pre-tested. The vehicle to be launched has an established trajectory and destination, and a cradle or derrick to steady it for the launch. So too with the launching of an adolescent into adulthood. The successful launch begins with the young child's successful navigation of the developmental trajectory as scripted by their genes and their society.

As I indicated in Chapter 4, "Children Playing and Learning," children, historically, learned adult skills and picked up knowledge of the culture (religion, kinship, manners, history, lore) through observing and eavesdropping. This gathered wisdom is then processed, applied, and retained by the child through make-believe play, and through practice with appropriate tools and materials. Adults implicitly signal their approval of the child's initiative by letting them use "real" tools, making scaled-down tools for them, or donating old tools, scraps of materials, and so on. Approval of the child's self-initiated efforts to learn is also conveyed by allowing them to quietly observe adult activity and, where feasible, letting them pitch in. Barbara Rogoff and her colleagues have documented this process—which they refer to as "learning by observing and pitching in" (LOPI)—for decades, across many villages in Mexico and Guatemala.

The child is clearly motivated to become competent, to master the skills of his/her seniors, paying great attention to older siblings as role models, for example. Parallel to this efficacy drive—which was first identified over fifty years ago—there is a complementary drive to "fit in." This latter is clearly shown in a landmark study which revealed children's eagerness to assist an adult in completing a project. This is one area where cultural anthropology and developmental psychology converge. Combining these insights, we can propose that the child has been prepared by evolutionary processes to discover its place in society and proceed to fill it to the approval and satisfaction of all. Children as young as three—if permitted—are already preparing to launch.

The essays in Chapters 4 and 5 highlight the breakdown of this self-starting and self-guided learning system in contemporary society. Children are no longer able to learn the culture through their own initiative. Artificial and not very effective means (e.g. teachers, textbooks, classrooms) have usurped the child's autonomy. Further, the child is no longer required to fit in; they get a free pass.

Where village children are eager and encouraged to "fit in" and move along a trajectory toward greater competence and responsibility, their "cosmopolitan" counterparts—second- and third-generation migrants from the village—are discouraged from following such a pattern. In a comparative (village versus urban migrants) study in Mexico, none of the middle-class urban kids volunteered to do chores or to help out:

> A mother reported: "I'll walk into the bathroom and everything is all soapy, and she says to me 'I'm just cleaning.' I tell her, 'You know what? It's better that you don't clean anything for me, because I'm going to slip and fall in here.'" ... [M]others in the cosmopolitan community did not allow their children to take care of younger siblings, stating that childcare is the parent's responsibility alone ... [another] mother reported, "I tell her, Don't take roles that are not yours, I tell her, Enjoy your childhood, you will be a Mom one day."

In many respects, children are actively discouraged from fitting in, being told they shouldn't "be like everyone else." Quite the opposite of fitting in, as with original names, children are encouraged to develop unique personalities, talents, and desires. Kusserow's ethnography of well-off families in New York City illustrates this phenomenon very well (all taken from A. S. Kusserow, *American*

Individualisms: Child Rearing and Social Class in Three Neighborhoods (New York: Palgrave Macmillan, 2004)):

- "It was quite evident that by age three Parkside children were already ... small but complete 'little people' with their own tastes, desires, needs, and wants."
- "My daughter is extraordinary at chess and ice skating, for which I pay through the nose."
- "As with Parkside parents, the importance of words in self-expression was emphasized in Parkside preschools."
- "Art was seen as a reflection of each child's unique personality, and thus the naming of one's work was paramount."

Cognitive scientist Chris Sinha tells a revealing story about taking his then seven-year-old daughter Kate to a Zapotec village in Mexico. Kate was invited to try her hand at making a pot. She duly emulated the potter's posture and her hand movements. Their lack of a common tongue was no problem as the potter expected Kate to learn by observing and replicating. Kate made an "original" pot that didn't closely match the model. The potter took the pot, squashed it, and remade it in the correct pattern (the villagers sell and use their ceramics). Kate was very upset and cried. The watching villagers couldn't understand why, especially as the potter indicated that, after firing, Kate could take home the now well-made pot. For Kate, the issue wasn't mastering pottery, but expressing her personality through a self-made object.

Our children are encouraged to discover their own talents rather than emulating others. Their horizons are without boundary, while village children focus their attention on the highly visible adult roles they are preparing to assume. While our children's make-believe play involves imaginary, storybook, or video game characters and plots, village children build dramas from the scenes around them.

In the village, this period of learning and helping voluntarily is succeeded in middle childhood (ages five to seven) by a period where the child, gradually, but not reluctantly, loses some of

Figure 7.3. Moroccan girl and mother in market

his/her autonomy. The chores that were done voluntarily and, perhaps, not quite up to adult standards are now "assigned" and must be done correctly. It is in middle childhood, in most societies, when adults recognize that the child has gained "sense"— which means maturity, judgment, a sense of responsibility, paying attention to what's relevant, and taking the initiative. There is now clear gender differentiation in chore assignments, clothing, and lifestyle. A girl spends her time in her mother's company as mommy's helper and apprentice (See Figure 7.3). She is very consciously observing how her mother does things and modifies her behavior accordingly. Boys, on the other hand, spend much more time in company with peers and older siblings. Their chores (herding, hunting) take them farther afield. To mark these changes, there may be minor rites of passage, such as presenting a boy with his own shepherd's crook, or acknowledging a girl's first salmon catch.

Note, however, that these changes from early to middle childhood are hardly drastic or abrupt. Girls have been observing their mothers closely since birth, and as soon as they are able they begin to emulate her, in play or "for real." Unless disabled, a child can't "fail." He/she just keeps on trying, at his/her own pace, until competent. Yukaghir (Siberian foragers) describe it as "doing is learning and learning is doing." There are very few decision points along the way. In a herding society, all boys herd; the older they are the bigger the flock. Or they may graduate from herding goats to herding camels. But other "careers" are not available to them.

As a child in the 1950s, I can recall that all my uncles worked in the "Tube Mill," a local factory under the aegis of U.S. Steel. All my male cousins followed their fathers into the mill. The sons of dry-goods-store owners joined the business. Farm kids became farmers. The sons of undertakers became undertakers. In the Middle Ages, among the landed class, the oldest son inherited the estate, the second oldest became an army or navy officer, and the third a clergyman. One's trajectory toward the goal of an adult place in society was pretty well fixed from birth. Failure to launch was not an issue.

The most important aspect of the transition to adolescence in the village is diminished involvement with peers. Children may be forced to go through elaborate and painful initiation rites, similar to the boot camp which precedes induction in the military. The message adolescents receive, whether during initiation or more informally, is that they must prepare to join the ranks of adult society. This means being able to produce sufficient food to support a family, build a house, and negotiate the right to land for farming, or acquire a boat to fish from. They know how to do all these things by this point, but now the stakes are higher. More attention is paid to their accomplishments rather than their skills. But, above all, adolescents must submit themselves to the authority of adults, and accept that their high standing among peers and youth of the community must give way to a very low rank among adults. If they acquiesce, they will enjoy an arranged marriage, paid for by kin. They will be given resources to establish a separate household. Others will donate their labor to help get the new adult launched.

At this point, I'll digress to address the first issue raised at the beginning of this essay. In general, anthropologists do *not* see any evidence of failure-to-launch syndrome, as just explained. The exceptions are very recent. The most commonly seen cases occur where schooling is introduced into the community and seduces everyone, especially young people, into believing that it will lead to riches, either directly in terms of wage employment "in the city," or indirectly, through the remittance of wages back to the village from the newly employed. As students, children may be relieved of a significant portion of their chores and/or exempted from learning the skill-craft associated with the local means of earning a livelihood. Of course, most of these aspirations are doomed to disappointment because the quality of schooling is often poor and salaried jobs are nonexistent. So, the adolescents who had been on an alternative trajectory leading to riches return to the village no richer and lacking the skills and the will to accept the demanding labor incorporated in the "normal" trajectory. Another, rarer situation occurs when outside forces (usually missionaries) disrupt traditional rituals. One casualty is the initiation rite, which is, as we've seen, considered critical in transitioning adolescents into their adult roles. Among the Bumbita Arapesh, for example, youth may no longer experience initiation into the Tambaran cult, and they are unable to learn the magic spells that are necessary "to produce thriving and abundant crops of yams," the staple food.

At about the age that adolescents in the village are being reeled in and socialized to take their place among adults, our youth are distancing themselves further from society. Automobiles, smartphones, part-time jobs, and the prevailing atmosphere of high school and college allow adolescents to retreat from the world at large into a distinct youth culture. Far from preparing youth to launch, this culture encourages the postponement of responsibility, career building, upward striving, and family formation.

Helicopter parents, refusing to "cut the cord," call college deans to complain about their son's B grade. But this approach inevitably backfires. When students suffer the natural consequences of their behaviors, they tend to develop the resiliency that is essential to a successful launch. Parents who step in to rescue them from a failing grade, an unfinished paper, or a penalty for misbehavior are creating a pattern that perpetuates a need for ongoing rescue. Children are not developing the skills they need to become fully functioning adults. It is no surprise then that, in the US at least, broad measures of preparedness for and graduation from college are in decline, particularly for males.

As with many of my university colleagues—among whom failure to launch is a favored topic—I have seen this phenomenon emerge and grow since I began my college teaching career in 1968. We now encounter an entirely new type of student—one to whom I may find myself delivering this homily: "If you'd spent as much time working on your assignment as you've spent lawyering me to raise your grade, we wouldn't be having this conversation." Those faculty who "hold the line" on course standards are vilified by many "straight-A" students who've never tasted failure. Those who surrender and teach "defensively" are guiltily aware of their culpability for the failure of poorly educated graduates to satisfy the minimal requirements for literacy and numeracy expected by employers. The consequences are not only individual. Failure to launch threatens the economy at large. US students are avoiding "hard" subjects like engineering and math, hence a growing and very significant portion of our engineers and scientists are "imported"—or the work is "outsourced" to other countries. Immigrants who did not shy away from "hard" subjects have gained expertise that affords them a much higher likelihood of earning a visa and good salary. Among skilled workers, the situation is little different. Native youth are spurning physically challenging "trades," so employers must draw on the pool of eager-to-work, eager-to-learn immigrants.

> more and more able-bodied men are out of work and are not even looking for work. These men aren't included in the unemployment statistics because they've given up looking for a job. They may be from middle-class families and many have some college education. Their ranks are growing rapidly . . . [as to working-class youth, a building contractor laments that] he can't find good help. "It's been

more than ten years since I've been able to hire any young man born in the US and keep him for more than a month. Number one, these young guys nowadays have no idea of craftsmanship. Number two, they don't have any interest in learning. None whatsoever."

Failure-to-launch syndrome is real; it is growing rapidly with no end in sight. I see it arising from a perfect storm created by our modern child-rearing philosophy. The symptoms first appear in infancy and grow more virulent throughout childhood and adolescence. Among these symptoms, I'd include:

- Parents see infants as all-absorbing of their time and attention. We may direct more speech to our speechless infants than to our spouses. Their many possessions—baby furniture, clothing, toys, and foods—"take over" a larger and larger portion of the domestic space.

- From birth, children are afforded very high status; they are not treated as incompetent, incomplete, or in the process of "becoming." Effectively, they start life on a pinnacle of love, approval, and admiration. There may be nowhere to go from there except downhill.

- Parents exhibit an urgency to create unique individuals who are directed to follow their own path rather than tread the well-worn paths of their predecessors. The path may turn out to be a long detour leading away from the launch pad, but that's OK with their family and friends.

- Parents grant children choices and don't impose obligations. They can choose not to do (or eat) anything they don't want to. They can avoid challenges or unfamiliar situations and take the path of least resistance.

- Parents treat the child's noncompliance or failure as situated in the teacher, the school, the peer group, or society at large. Our children are "special" and should not be held to the standards that apply to other children. On the other hand, they are not to be denied the opportunities afforded to their peers, regardless of their worthiness in others' eyes. Slow, unmotivated, and cranky soccer players *must* be accorded the same amount of game time as everyone else.

- Helicopter parents hover within reach, ready to swoop down and morph into snowplows clearing all obstacles in the child's path.

- Parents worry about damage to the child's self-esteem and act to shield the child from the consequences of stupidity, failure, or non-conformity.

- Our "special" children do not need to conform to social rules. They are given a pass on etiquette, politeness, and co-operation. They learn to ask and take from others—not to give. They have difficulty accepting the subordinate role of apprentice or employee and adhering to routines and following directions.

- Children lack a sense of obligation and sympathy toward others because parents don't ask it of them. The disappearance of household chores is one result. An inability to work co-operatively in a team situation is another.

- Parents invest greater and greater sums to satisfy their child's every want. In the process, children are permitted to withdraw into the narrow society of their peers, or even narrower society afforded by social media. They are dependents who behave independently. They enjoy an artificially elevated living standard and have difficulty adjusting to the lifestyle afforded by an assistant's or a trainee's salary.

Taken together, these child-rearing practices may not lead to a successful launch. Instead of a careful trajectory from helplessness and incompetence to the confidence, knowledge, and focus of a job and family, these practices and attitudes lead to the creation of parasites. What might be the antidote? Many more challenges, much less supervision.

8   Summary and Speculation

I would first reiterate one of the primary goals of this book. I am very concerned about the ready ascription of failure or inadequacy to parents. The root of this problem lies with our contemporary culture's false understanding of what is "normal" in parenting and child development. Childhood, as we now know it, is a thoroughly modern invention. It is a gigantic experiment in which current ideas and strategies for child rearing are unprecedented. By reviewing patterns gleaned from anthropology and history, I hope to redefine what is "normal" or common in order to demonstrate how extraordinary our contemporary expectations for parents and their children are.

Models for Raising Children: What Are the Major Differences?

Throughout this book, I have drawn contrasts between the WEIRD childhood depicted in our common understanding (and, to a great extent, in the pages of child-development texts) and what one sees in the ethnographic and historic records. I will summarize these discussions through a series of polemical comparisons which follow.

1. Parenting guides are written for parents who live in a society where the child's well-being is paramount; its needs trump those of other family members. In the societies studied by anthropologists and historians, children are the lowest-ranking members of the community and are treated accordingly, fed on leftovers from the adult's meal, for example. The underlying "theory" is that older people know more; they've

had more experiences; they've worked hard; they've borne, cared for, and fed their children; and they've suffered, so, of course, they are entitled to respect and preferential treatment. Children accrue a moral debt since they can't take care of themselves and must rely upon others. It will be many years before their moral credit offsets their debt.

2. In the twenty-first century, infants are invested with tremendous inherent worth. Millions are spent on enhanced reproductive techniques and millions more on keeping alive even the earliest preterm neonates. This is a striking contrast with our predecessors' priorities. Since the dawn of the species, humans have abandoned or disposed of surplus or defective babies. Girl babies were (and still are) especially vulnerable to population-limiting choices. Societies developed elaborate customs that legitimated and dignified these practices, such as treating an anomalous infant as a changeling. As these practices were, eventually, condemned by moral authorities, unwanted babies were consigned to institutional care (church-run hospitals, nunneries) where the majority perished. While infanticide is now universally condemned, it undoubtedly continues in impoverished communities. Less dramatically, we can see parents making difficult choices regarding which of their offspring should receive costly (by their standards) medical care. Similar decisions are made in terms of children's schooling versus working to support the family. These extremes of blank-check, cost-is-no-object valuation of every fetus and infant versus the unavoidable triage practiced by the poor are both deserving of close moral and fiscal scrutiny. Surely the drastic imbalance in investment requires some adjusting?

3. Our society sees each child as a treasure with great emotional value to the new parents. The family fully expects to provide care and resources to each child well past puberty. Children are precious and innocent, needing protection from the world of adults and exploitative labor. With the significant exception of nomadic foraging peoples, children were considered

chattel, the property of their parents. As such, they could be sold or donated to another family or to the church. In early industrialized societies, children were employed—to enhance the family's earnings—from an early age. Today, a very large segment of the world's peoples still holds the expectation that the child will participate in the household economy as their maturity level permits. Children of ten years of age may be doing a "full day's work." In many agrarian societies, the child is able to provide a surplus of calories or "return" on its parents' investment. Adults may celebrate the child's accomplishments *as a worker.* Childhood might be described as "brief."

4. Most modern societies embrace the ideal of limited fertility so that one can "afford" the high costs of raising (few) children. In the past, and in much of the world that still practices subsistence agriculture, high fertility—especially the production of males—is highly valued, even if children may not be. Childless individuals may be scorned or suspected of witchcraft.

5. We celebrate the child's birth with baby showers, newly decorated nurseries, family gatherings, and christenings. Anxiety about the delivery and possible negative outcomes is almost nonexistent. In societies where infant and maternal mortality rates are high, the mother and baby are in a liminal state, vulnerable to infection and other medical crises, as well as to potential harm to and from others. Birth and the postpartum period may be characterized by secrecy and seclusion.

6. Among the well educated, a baby is treated as a sentient being from birth, a worthy target of speech, capable of responding, if nonverbally. Indeed, in East Asia and among the Western elite, the fetus may be seen as capable of responding to speech and music. More commonly throughout the world, the infant provokes mixed emotions and ambiguity. High infant mortality and threats to the mother's life cast a pall. The incontinent infant—lacking hair, speech,

pigmentation, motor control—is not seen as a person. Personhood may be delayed for months or years. But babies aren't just nonpersons. Elaborate theories exist that account for the liminal state of the infant and prescribe steps to be taken to insure the child properly "ripens."

7. The modern "ideal" family features the biological parents and their children cohabiting under one roof. The parents, faithful to each other, co-operate fully in the household economy and share the great burden of child rearing. This perspective can be juxtaposed with growing evidence that, from the beginning of humankind and across the world, men rarely commit to lifelong monogamy, may not reside with their wives and offspring, and, hence, may have virtually no contact with their children. The "nuclear" family is relatively rare; far more common are large extended families and households composed of mother and offspring. Polygyny, or families composed of a husband and two or more wives, is extremely common—at least as a cultural ideal. Statistically, the modern family is, increasingly, composed of a single, usually female, head and her children. There's no evidence that any of these family patterns is, by definition, more "natural."

8. We regulate many aspects of our infants' and young children's lives, including creating a unique environment for them—cribs, nurseries, high chairs. We regulate where and when they eat and sleep. On the other hand, we make many adjustments in our schedule of activities to ensure they are kept stimulated and engaged. More typically, there are no separate eating or sleeping arrangements for children. Infants sleep with their mothers and are fed on demand, around the clock. Toddlers feed opportunistically and/or when others are eating. Although there may be special "weaning" foods, the child quickly transitions to the same diet as everyone else. The infant's basic needs are taken care of promptly, but otherwise they are largely ignored.

9. We treat the child's illness as a strictly *medical* problem. Modern vaccinations and treatments have reduced infant

mortality to insignificant levels. In the village, folk medic-
aments that often do more harm than good, chronic infection
and malnutrition, and the lack of vaccinations maintain
infant/child mortality at high levels. Because these problems
occur so frequently, parents may not respond with great
urgency. Illness is often seen as originating in supernatural
forces or familial discord, particularly between spouses or
between a wife and her mother-in-law. The "folk" treatments
provided by a shaman or healer may focus on these issues.
This must be diagnosed and remediated before the child can
get well. Based on modern medical understanding, these
diagnoses of illness arising from discord and the subsequent
"prescriptions" may be quite efficacious, as we now know that
high levels of family stress are detrimental to children.

10. Especially in recent years, sex and biological relatedness have
become far less critical in judging a child's value to its parents.
Girls are now welcomed and the adoption of unrelated children is common. This is one among many examples from our
culture where we oppose or discount our evolutionary heri-
tage. In more traditional communities, relatedness and sex
remain important criteria in determining whether the newborn is celebrated or disposed of. Children are adopted by
kin, only rarely by unrelated individuals. It may be helpful to
note that children are only so malleable, their personality and
"nature" set more by genes than by "upbringing." Likewise,
while there may be a universal, biological need to "parent" or
care for children, this need must be attenuated, if not absent
altogether, where there is no genetic link between parent
and child.

11. In traditional societies, mothers pass off their infants and
toddlers to sibling or granny caretakers. The mother's ener-
gies are, preferentially, devoted to subsistence or commercial
activity and to preparing herself for the next birth. In the
West and in East Asia, one commonly finds selfless mothers
who lavish attention and instruction on their young well into
adolescence. Debates rage regarding the potential harm done

to the child when the mother works outside the home. On the morning I wrote this, the newspaper reported Turkish President Erdoğan's sermon in which he castigated women as "deficient" if they'd borne fewer than three children or refused to remain homebound mothers.

12. Among the well educated, there is the presumption that, to mature successfully, children require intellectual stimulation from birth—or even in the womb. Their caretakers aim to "optimize" the child's development to maximize their accomplishments. This perspective can be challenged by the belief that children are without sense or the ability to learn until at least their fifth year. They are, in effect, unteachable. In lieu of stimulating and engaging babies, childcare methods emphasize keeping it in a quiescent state to reduce risk and the burden of care. Swaddling, carrying the child in a sling, and using a cradle aid this effort.

13. We have very low expectations for our children to assist us in our work, household duties, and care of family members. They are free to play or attend school. Village children eagerly participate in "chores," particularly the care of younger siblings—a role which little girls relish. This sharp contrast may account for diminished pro-social behavior, lack of a sense of obligation and responsibility, and poor work ethic in our offspring.

14. We don't always expect grandparents to be involved in childcare, particularly when they don't reside with or near the family. In the village, grannies play a critical role in childcare, particularly the care and emotional support of recently weaned children.

15. Throughout much of human history, fathers rarely contribute to childcare and there may be specific prohibitions on any close contact between fathers and their offspring. *We* do expect fathers to participate in childcare and, unfortunately, there is a persistent gap between mothers' and fathers' expectations of paternal involvement in childcare and household routines. The gap is closing in many highly

modern, progressive societies, but this issue remains a point of contention and may contribute to the decision to divorce.

16. We think babies are "adorable"—even "terrible two-year-olds" can be "cute." Many societies, in contrast, practice "toddler rejection," where the recently weaned and cranky child is banned from the breast and sent to grandma's or to play with older siblings. The recalcitrant child may be treated harshly by everyone, in spite of dramatic tantrums. Indeed, mothers who devote "excess" attention to their weanlings are chastised as creating an overly dependent and weak child.

17. There is considerable anguish and debate—at least in the US—regarding the role of professional child-caretakers such as nannies, preschool teachers, and *au pairs*. Claims are made about the harm done to children being cared for by someone other than their mother. Historically, women have almost always availed themselves of professionals, if they could afford it. These included wet nurses, nannies, pedagogues, and tutors.

18. Annually, there is a flood of volumes and new websites devoted to authoritative, "scientific" coverage of the child's development and appropriate, *essential* parenting practices. They appear in response to the voracious demand from anxious parents for guidance and "foolproof" practices to "fix" their child. Many, if not most, of these ideas are novel and untried from a historical and cross-cultural perspective. In small-scale, face-to-face societies—especially where older siblings are part-time alloparents—one acquires a model of correct child rearing from observing others and through direct, supervised practice. There is, effectively, no debate or controversy as everyone is expected to follow their "customs." Likewise, "problem" children also tend to eventually fall in line to avoid being ignored or neglected.

19. We invest a great deal of time in socializing our children through conversations. The intent is to instruct children by precept and persuasion, not punishment. Another acceptable behavior-management tactic is to withhold or grant some

favorite resource, such as access to electronic media, but this clearly is not a cure-all. Corporal punishment is seen as a retrograde strategy for socializing the young and may be prohibited by law. Relatively speaking, villagers avoid interfering with children's autonomy, expecting them to *want* to fit in and learn their culture. If the child deviates from expectations, brief and sometimes angry directives are used to correct. Other harsh correction tactics may include frightening the child or corporal punishment. Parents who don't discipline their children are pilloried. In East Asia, parents still rely heavily on shaming the child into compliance, but this tactic is also largely taboo in the West. These coercive tactics were effective. Managing the child's behavior largely through reasoned speech requires a substantial investment in moving the child as rapidly as possible into adult levels of language, manners, and sense of responsibility. It's a bit like the purpose and operation of "finishing schools."

20. Much of adult culture, including work, food acquisition, sex, and entertainment is restricted. Our children are perceived as too young, sensitive, or vulnerable to be readily admitted to the adult sphere. On the other hand, parents take special pains to spend "quality time" participating in the child's world. Dinner table conversations, for example, at least in the US, may be child- rather than adult-centered. Parents "play" with their children in a great variety of contexts (make-believe, games, "roughhousing"). In the village, adult lives are an open book to be read and learned. The children's world is generally devoid of adult participation. Adult–child "conversation" would be unseemly. Children are tolerated in adult company if they remain undemanding and unobtrusive. Children learn a great deal from observing other family members as they work, prepare and eat meals, and do craftwork. An exception to this pattern may be found in hunting and gathering societies where very young children may be unwelcome on foraging and hunting expeditions. I think we can borrow at least one of these ideas, namely that children

are tolerated in adult company and can observe and learn, but should remain unobtrusive. The problem with allowing a child to engage with adults in a social gathering is that the setting shifts from an adult-oriented setting (from which the child learns about "grown-ups") to a child-oriented one. There's a fine line here where a "mature," well-mannered child can profitably participate in an adult gathering as long as it remains an *adult* gathering.

21. We are leery of our children's peers, fearing their "bad influence." We isolate our children in the home and carefully select peers to invite for "playdates" and "sleepovers." We choose to enroll our children in particular schools, associations, and sports teams. Village children are incorporated into the neighborhood peer group from a very early age. They spend far more time in the company of, being cared for, and learning from peers than parents. What socialization opportunities are lost when all a child's peers are cautiously "vetted" and they may only associate with the "right" kids?

22. In the neontocracy, the child is given an almost inexhaustible supply of social capital and does very little to earn it. Deference to strangers, those older, kin, and parents is either not expected at all (in the US), or inculcated at a relatively late age. The same would be true for behavior in public places. In the gerontocracy, children occupy the lowest rank and must early on—sometimes via explicit instruction—learn to behave correctly with others, including, especially, sharing. Correct kin terms and terms of address that reflect relative rank are drummed into the very young. Many postindustrial societies such as France, Japan, and Korea still socialize children in good manners, including table manners, and proper speech and behavior toward others—particularly adults.

23. Aggressive behavior by children, including verbal aggression, is tolerated less and less in Western society. Such behavior is considered harmful to the less aggressive, less popular children. Cross-culturally, there is great variability in the tolerance for aggression. This ranges from societies that actively

promote aggressive behavior—of future warriors—or suppress the behavior in keeping with a low-conflict, egalitarian ethos. However, most societies tolerate and expect children to engage in rough boisterous play and verbal dueling and teasing.

24. Contemporary values in modernized societies stress the malleability of gender roles—girls are encouraged to pursue everything from contact sports to careers in politics. More typically, we see extremely rigid management of the development of gender roles; the daughter becomes a full-time assistant to her mother, and boys may endure a painful initiation to divest them, forcibly, of any feminine traits acquired from their mothers. In my view, this is one, unequivocally positive, change in how contemporary society looks at childhood.

25. The average child in the neontocracy has access to many safe and "educational" toys but may lose interest in them quickly. Toys are subject to fashion and fad. In the gerontocracy, the very young play mostly with found objects, such as tools and utensils. These may include sharp knives and other "dangerous" items. While the risks are acknowledged, the assumption is that the child will only learn to use the object by *actually* using it, clumsily at first, but then with greater precision. My own feeling is that children benefit from "creating" or inventing their playthings. This might simply involve "borrowing" a broom, some pots and pans, or clothes from the laundry basket for dress-up. Large, empty cardboard boxes have unlimited potential.

26. In recent years, play in the West (especially in the US) has rapidly changed. There is much greater adult involvement in children's play, ranging from the infant exploring novel objects (guided by a parent) to children participating in football (soccer) that is managed by parents, coaches, and referees. Rules are designed to be learned and then adhered to. Traditionally, children's play is unmediated by parents, coaches, strict rules, structured playing fields, or "regulation" equipment. Children have free rein to utilize the traditional

accoutrements of game play—customary rules, homemade marbles, chalked lines on sidewalks, scavenged play materials, the language of the game, etc.—and to modify them as the occasion warrants. This ad hoc process facilitates the development of "gamesmanship"—the ability to manipulate social relations during play to maximize the satisfaction of the players, as well as the payoffs to the "best" players. Being "the best" might not just mean being a consistent winner, but being someone that others are eager to play with.

27. Make-believe play is valued as a learning medium in nearly all cultures. In ours, parents become actively engaged with children's make-believe in purchasing or making appropriate props; in guiding the child's development in make-believe and fantasy; in linking make-believe to reading, books, and stories; and in using the medium pedantically to teach moral and other lessons. When we don't intervene to guide play, our children have a tendency to become bored. Village parents get involved in make-believe only to the extent of donating materials, including miniature or cast-off tools. Otherwise, they keep their distance. Make-believe in the village, lacking these external fantasy sources, is firmly rooted in the real world that children can readily observe. There are few or no taboo subjects; children may act out relations between the sexes and religious rites. Inventiveness is evident in the construction of scripts, the scavenging of props, and the assignment of roles and personalities to players. Some of the most memorable play episodes recorded by anthropologists show children successfully parodying adult behavior and discourse. Boredom seems unknown.

28. Today there is also much greater solitary play since families are smaller and neighborhoods are "dangerous." Much of this play is now conducted via electronic media. The quintessential play experience takes place within an enduring and ubiquitous village or neighborhood playgroup. The composition of the group might be mixed with respect to age and gender, at least for children aged five and under. The children's play

space was/is the community as a whole, considered safe under the watchful attention of older neighbors. All play is active and profoundly social. Our children need many more opportunities to play and interact in a mixed-age cohort of children rather than being restricted to same-age playmates. We also need to fight back against the paranoia that sees any unsupervised play setting as threatening.

29. In the family context, the roles of mothers, fathers, and children tend to be quite different. Each operates separately, in a distinct sphere of activity. The kitchen is the mother's domain, father owns the "den," and each child occupies his/her bedroom. Village family members, regardless of age, participate in many of the same suite of activities, in the same physical spaces (fields, garden, kitchen). Differentiation occurs in terms of more specific tasks or subcomponents of the tasks. These may be identified as male or female responsibilities. They may be broken down into easier or more complex tasks apportioned on the basis of maturity and competence (sweeping the floor versus doing the laundry). We tend to think of "family activities" as happening within the context of leisure or recreational settings only. Shared work is infrequent. In church, parents attend the "service," while children are in Sunday school.

30. Throughout ethnographic literature, formal schooling is virtually absent. Children are supposed to learn the culture through observation and imitation. Teaching is seen as unnecessary and a waste of an adult's precious time. Children are avid spectators and this trait is considered the basis for the child's acquisition of her culture. Instead of focusing attention only on one's teacher or a parent acting as teacher, village children display a broad awareness of all that's going on around them. Children are seen to acquire "sense," or the ability to learn, from example and to adjust behavior in accord with adult expectations, around the age of five to seven. "Intelligence" is not conceived of as cleverness and verbal knowledge, but as compliance with and

awareness of the expectations of others. It is the ability to be a positive contributor to family life and subsistence. "Independence" doesn't mean having one's own opinions and possessions, but being self-sufficient and not making demands on others. Our recent history shows formal, highly verbal schooling starting in early childhood and lasting into adulthood. We might think of pedagogy as a menu of tools and strategies for bringing the child from a state of ignorance to a state of knowledge. Almost every item on such a menu would be of relatively recent vintage. In fact, the complete novelty of classroom instruction may account, in part, for the apparent failure of so many students, teachers, and educational innovations. (Does anyone remember *New Math*?)

31. Given the predominance of "standards" and "standardized" in discussions of contemporary schooling, there may be the perception that schools are as mechanized as factories. The impression is created that managers—by imposing standards, lesson plans, curricula, and rules—will produce the desired outcomes in terms of teacher and student behaviors. From the studies of anthropologists, it is patently clear that schooling outcomes are affected mostly by the surrounding cultural context. The child's home experiences, the local community's expectations for the school, economic opportunities post-schooling, and the funding available (to pay teachers, for example) are among the many factors that contribute to the mix. The primary contribution that child psychology makes to these outcomes is the finding that the skills and knowledge transmitted through the curriculum are cumulative. That is, children who are academically able in kindergarten will be academically able as college freshmen.

32. Since G. Stanley Hall published his monumental work on adolescence at the end of the nineteenth century, the educated public in the West has accepted several broad generalizations about the nature of adolescence. These include conflict over sexuality, a "generation gap," and a difficult or

even traumatic transition to adulthood. Such generalizations have been challenged by anthropologists, beginning with Margaret Mead's classic *Coming of Age in Samoa* in 1928. We discover many societies where sexual relations begin early and without drama. Similarly, adolescence may be quite short as mature, hardworking children move, seamlessly, into their adult roles. Adolescent–parent conflict is not a given. In East Asia, children are raised to respect and appreciate their parents, sublimating their will to their parents'. This successful cultivation of filial affection and, later, responsibility carries right on through adulthood. But anthropology also confirms the existence of very widespread and likely inherited commonalities shared by adolescents, such as heightened risk-taking, sexual desire, and the tendency for adolescent males to cluster in "gangs."

33. In WEIRD societies, intervention may be necessary to resolve adolescent psychological conflicts and disabilities. Suicide rates spike. Counseling and psychotropic drugs may be prescribed to reduce stress and "acting-out" behaviors. Elsewhere, the "problems" of adolescence are considered largely behavioral. Dramatic, painful, and demanding initiation rites may be "prescribed" as the remedy to correct antisocial behavior and bring youth in line with adult expectations. A significant element may be to indoctrinate initiates for their new roles as young adults. As such, they gain opportunities such as marriage and the resources to form a family. But they also lose their autonomy and must now display proper subordination vis-à-vis older community members. Could it be that our adolescents are "stressed" because there is no longer any automatic, expected, and well-prepared-for transition to adulthood? Or, could the problem be that we hold so few expectations for children to "conform," to "act responsibly," to diligently pursue education and career, and to commit to a lasting relationship that, when they reach the age where the adult role is finally thrust on them, they're woefully unprepared?

34. We believe that the child's "normal" state is one of happiness, and act vigorously to alleviate any symptoms of unhappiness. Given the child's low status, and lack of skills and resources, village parents would wonder why s/he should be happy. Consider also the likelihood of malnutrition, infection, and chronic illness. Unhappiness is to be expected, and when we see village children who are obviously joyful in spite of all, we marvel at their resiliency. Would that we acknowledged such resiliency in our overprotected (and -medicated) cherubs.

Gazing into the Crystal Ball

In conclusion, I'll offer up some very personal and speculative ideas about the future of parenthood.

The US will continue to be an innovator and leader, for good or ill, in childcare and child-rearing practices, including passing fads and fashions. This is the case because (a) US parents can afford it, and (b) in the rest of the postindustrial world, childcare is highly managed by government. That is, comparable, well-off countries see childcare and child rearing as instruments of public and economic policy, just as they view schooling. Cultural practices that used to be driven by tradition or folk culture are now driven by "experts" guiding government policy.

The emphasis on individualism (see Chapter 7) characteristic of the US and, to a lesser extent, Western Europe will continue to apply to both children and their parents. From obstetric procedures and health care decisions, to day care, to diet, to child media programming, US policies leave parents free to follow their own inspirations—regardless of the cost to themselves, insurance providers, and taxpayers. In contrast, China, for instance, is committed to expanding its economy—freeing itself from a reliance on farming and heavy industry—in order to compete in the knowledge economy. To do that, it will pull out all the stops to ensure that parents' contribution to the modern economy is not disrupted by the burden of childcare.

Hence there will be all-day nursery school for two-year-olds, and "full-time moms" will be considered anomalous.

In the less developed nations, one's education will continue to be a critical factor in the fate of children. For a long time, there has been a "movement" to ensure equal access to schooling for women and men, but traditional cultural forces have offered concerted resistance. Daily headlines from the Muslim world remind us that there is very strong opposition to the ideas of education, employment, and social life outside the home for millions of Muslim women. Schooling for girls is a direct threat to male hegemony; that's why Malala was a target and why she's become such a potent symbol.

Poverty, non-mechanized and labor-intensive farming, and rural isolation also severely limit women's schooling. It turns out, however, that even a few years of education can make a measurable difference in how women approach childbearing and child rearing. LeVine and colleagues' aggregate results from studying several less developed countries support the notion that even a few years of schooling can "modernize" a woman's approach to her own fertility (reducing it), and improve her ability to keep her offspring alive and healthy. Even rudimentary, school-acquired literacy has a consistent positive effect on the comprehension of public-service radio messages. Mothers who'd had some schooling delivered more intelligible and complete illness narratives when presenting their sick children to a clinic attendant. Minimally educated mothers "internalize the teacher role from experience in Western-type schools and use it as mothers." Worldwide, surveys have shown that children's prospects are improved if their mothers have been schooled.

In the introductory chapter, I presented my neontocracy-versus-gerontocracy polemic. Although the world is slowly moving toward a neontocracy, especially in economically developed nations, many countries are not. Corruption, surprisingly, is a major factor because, in a gerontocracy, children are at the bottom of the heap; they are treated as chattel. So, to the extent that corruption effectively skims the cream off the economy and off government services, very few benefits trickle down to children. If you want to know which nations will be making future progress on maternal–child health, education, and welfare issues, look for those where corruption is easing or is less entrenched.

I've become increasingly aware of an excruciating paradox with respect to parenting. As this book stresses, we can identify many situations in economically prosperous families of "over-parenting." Children may be overfed, over-scheduled, overindulged, expensively clothed and entertained, overmedicated and so on. In contrast, among the poorest and most unstable communities in the world, children aren't over-parented; they aren't parented at all. Consider the millions of refugee children produced by sectarian conflicts; child combatants in those conflicts; children orphaned by the AIDS epidemic; child slaves; child laborers; and street children who've escaped from meager diets, hard work, and abuse at home. In spite of much handwringing by reformers and child advocates, I see little abatement in either trend in the short term.

If I focus strictly on children growing up in the top echelon of society, I see a new profession emerging—the super-nanny (SN). The SN won't simply, or even primarily, take care of children; she/he will be someone with a college degree whose services resemble those of a wedding planner. The super-nanny will be a consultant who recommends reputable childcare services, and advises on schools, private tutors, music teachers, pediatricians, sports teams. The SN will assist in orchestrating the child's movement among all these activities. The super-nanny will stand in for parents preparing meals, supervising homework, and the like. Super-nannies will arise because parents are running themselves ragged trying to have a personal life, pursue a career, or just hold a full-time job *and* facilitate their children's manifold activities—which have become "essential." The most frequent lament on parenting blogs is that parents, mostly mothers, have painted themselves into a corner. Super-nanny to the rescue!

And if the cost of an SN is out of reach, I would urge parents to re-examine their priorities. When we try to enrich and fulfill our children's lives, the extravagant time and money expended will threaten our own well-being and emotional health. And we have increasing evidence that children are harmed in myriad ways by living in a stressed-out home.

Many parenting issues will remain highly contentious, and the resolutions are elusive. There is a growing and very persuasive cadre of scholars, child advocates, and bloggers who are vigorously lobbying on behalf of more lightly supervised playtime for children. These clarion calls ring out in favor of "free play" at home, play outside, more playful preschools and kindergartens, and a return of recess and guided play (in modern playgrounds with resident coaches) for children who've never learned social play. Weaker but persistent voices would weave play into classroom pedagogy. Others argue for more vigorous, risky play free of overly cautious caretakers. Many cite Finland as a shining example. But there are strong countervailing trends that aren't necessarily anti-play, but which achieve that effect as a by-product. These include the increasing concern for giving children a "head start" on later academic challenges, leading to more desk time, which in turn contributes to the obesity epidemic. Second, there is the threat of liability lawsuits in response to routine injuries on playgrounds and school facilities.

In a related trend, critics of over-scheduling have found allies among psychologists who have studied the benefits of unstructured downtime. The argument goes that boredom is good for kids. Boredom is the first step in transferring the child's need for interesting and enjoyable pursuits and activities from the parent to the child. Boredom provokes creativity, initiative, and contemplation. As adults, we pay big money for yoga instructors to teach us how to chill out; children are born with the capacity. My mother loved to tell visitors about an episode in my early childhood (interesting how one's lens on the earliest stages of life is the narratives told by parents and siblings who supply the text our own memories lack): we lived in a lovely, rural area and our house bordered a river. Apparently, I could spend up to an hour sitting on the bank just watching the river and the movement of the big maples on the bank. When asked what I was doing, I replied "watching the 'flections."

One insidious trend that continues unabated—defying science and logic—is the search, almost alchemist-like, for quick fixes to widespread challenges of raising children, such as inadequate academic performance. Even presidents have gotten in on the act (George W. Bush's "No Child Left Behind," Barack Obama's "Race to the Top"). The latest such magic bullet is something called "Grit." This is a movement that promotes a distillation of the essence of success (sports heroes are held up as exemplars) which turns out to be perseverance or "grit," and then tries to inoculate young children and students with this miracle vaccination. But, surely, perseverance is more likely to develop when children are freed from adult "instruction" and left to succeed or fail based on their own motivation and persistence? Will yet another "classroom intervention" not be counterproductive? David Denby dissects "Grit" and shows the potential for causing more harm than good. He laments that some public schools are now altering their curricula to teach grit and other gritty character traits. In California, a few schools are actually *grading* kids on grit (OMG).

The problem of child obesity will get much worse before it gets better. But, if a recent study of infants' food exposure is picked up in the blogosphere, there may be a ray of hope. Let me explain: in the "Trash Talking or Taking Out the Trash" essay in Chapter 7, I postulate that there might be a critical window of opportunity to teach young children the pro-social practice of "doing chores." Similarly, researchers have found a "flavor window" in infants from four to eighteen months of age. The more varied the child's diet during this period, the less likely they are to veto "healthy foods" when they're older. Bring on the puréed veggies!

It is hard to feel any sense of optimism regarding another, uniquely American, epidemic—the proliferation of lethal weapons. Children are particularly vulnerable. Although the vast majority of

US citizens favor more thorough screening of gun buyers for mental illness and prior history of violence, and of those on the terrorist watch list, the carnage continues with no legislative action—even after twenty first-graders were gunned down at an elementary school by a deranged twenty-year-old. Since 9/11, far more Americans have been killed by toddlers using guns than by terrorists. The number of such shootings by toddlers is climbing steadily and stands at nearly six per month. And the latest statistics show that across the US one child will be killed by a gun, on average, every other day.

I offer an optimistic forecast re the "Mommy Wars." I predict that they will wind down peacefully. Women's conflict over life choices will diminish for several reasons. One, they will be less and less likely to feel that they have choices. Single moms (a rapidly growing demographic) certainly, but married women as well, will feel compelled to work out of economic necessity. And, if working seems inevitable, certainly women will set their sights higher and higher. College will become a necessity—in the US, more women now graduate from college than men—and postgraduate study (MBA, MD, JD) more likely. Indebtedness, as the price for joining or remaining in the middle class, will reinforce women's need to work. The jury is still out, but there is growing consensus that fathers *should* assume a much greater share of childcare—and many actually are stepping up. The age at first pregnancy will continue to rise as fertility falls; women will have fewer and fewer children, later and later in their lifetime. No longer relying upon letting nature take its course, the decision to have a child or children will become the weightiest of people's lives.

Unfortunately, the Mommy Wars may be succeeded by a broad tug-of-war between Too Much and Not Enough (Dr. Seuss would love it) parenting. With this book, I hope to provide some tools for diplomacy in this emerging conflict.

9   The Backstory

My fifteen minutes of fame occurred in July 2007. A month earlier I'd published an academic article with the forgettable title (the editors rejected a snappier one) "Accounting for Variability in Mother–Child Play." Chris Shea, an enterprising essayist, picked up on the article and used it in a very provocative *Boston Globe* column with the marquee-worthy title "Leave the Kids Alone." My phone rang quite a bit in the ensuing weeks, and I participated as a guest in numerous, respectable, radio call-in shows here and abroad, including Brian Lehrer's show on WNYC. Shea's takeaway message from my article was that parent–child play had been drastically oversold. I certainly hadn't argued that it was necessarily a bad thing, but that we shouldn't be alarmed by its absence, or fear for the mother's or child's psyche. I also expressed concern about the public promotion of parent–child play in other societies and strata of our own society where it is absent.

The thesis of my article—buttressed by many sources—was that, throughout history and in the majority of the world's cultures, adults rarely play with children. Indeed, there are many societies, carefully described by anthropologists, where babies are fed on demand, protected from danger and the elements, but not talked to or played with—and they turn out just fine. I suggested that in the last two decades, nurture had turned into nature. That is, the childcare practices of the dominant culture had become "natural." Child psychologists, textbook authors, policy makers, and granting-agency personnel all belong to that dominant culture and tend to see its practices and their behavior as "normal." However, if childhood is viewed using a multicultural lens, a very different picture emerges.

Fame was fleeting, of course, and I kept my day job, continuing to research and write about children and culture in an academic vein. But I had been rewarded by the expressions of relief and gratitude from many parents who called in or posted to the shows' websites. These parents had been feeling guilty about not playing more with their children or, worse, not enjoying it when they did. There were also many comments from members of my generation (really old) to the effect that, "My parents never played with me, nor did the parents of my peers play with their children," thus affirming my claim that this was a very recent phenomenon.

Of course, parent–child play is not the only innovation in the culture of childhood. Another change—not necessarily an improvement—has been the diminution in children's free play in the outdoors. In 2010, I was invited to speak at a symposium organized by the Evolution Institute at Binghamton University on the theme Restoring Outdoor Play. One of the co-organizers, Peter Gray, writes a *Psychology Today* blog called "Freedom to Learn," and one of the featured presenters was Hara Estroff Murano, author of *A Nation of Wimps*, and associate editor of *Psychology Today*.

There was some very good chemistry at work as scholars and reformers found common ground at the symposium. I came away with the conviction that there were lessons for modern parents in the parenting practices of indigenous peoples—something I've studied for over forty years. Hara Murano graciously offered me a slot on the *Psychology Today* website to do a blog of my own. Casting about for a suitable name, it struck me that the major difference between the lives of village kids and those of our cherubs is that the former have so much more freedom. From our perspective, this freedom may seem like parental neglect. But, as little harm occurs, and, in fact, a great deal of good comes from this freedom, I thought the phrase "Benign Neglect" would serve nicely as the title for the blog.

My study and analysis of play cross-culturally—in part to debunk current popular dogma—spawned a much broader undertaking. I reasoned that, if something as vital and universal as play could be illuminated by a review of children's play in many other societies, what other pressing topics in child-development theory might be similarly examined? The book that ensued from this enterprise was published in late 2008 under the title *The Anthropology of Childhood: Cherubs, Chattel, Changelings*. Written as a scholarly tome, and a text-book for my class on the anthropology of childhood, the book met those objectives. But it was not written for a "lay audience" and, hence, the impact was limited. Other authors writing for parents and the general public, such as Lenore Skenazy, Mei-Ling Hopgood, and Christine Gross-Loh, did, however, borrow many of the arguments from the book, and these works pro-vided some of the impetus for *Raising Children: Surprising Insights from Other Cultures*.

With the publication of the second edition of my book *The Anthropology of Childhood*, I was granted fifteen more minutes of fame. This arose as a result of another fine article, this one by Michael Erard. Michael published a very personal review ("The Only Baby Book You'll Ever Need") of the book in the January 13, 2015, issue of the *New York Times*. It became—for a 500+ page academic tome—a best seller. This unexpected event led the publisher, Cambridge University Press, to propose that I write a nonacademic "baby" version of the longer text. This new book would be primarily aimed at parents, and perhaps also college students studying family and human development. As I was already committed to writing another book and several articles, I hesitated to accept. But my wife (and muse), Joyce Kinkead, suggested that I turn my blog posts into a book, reasoning that quite a few recent books started life as blogs. My *Psychology Today* posts were designed with the same goal as the proposed book. That is, they were written for parents and designed to provide colorful but insightful extracts from anthropology and history on the subject of children and parenting. And, of course, I always accept Joyce's suggestions because she's a lot smarter, so here we are.

How Did I Get Here?

I was born and raised in the country—rural Pennsylvania just northeast of Pittsburgh. Growing up, I can count on one hand the number of times I was taken to or visited the big city. One college summer I worked as a Fuller Brush salesman, traveling back roads on a Vespa. Some of my customers were old-order Amish farmers. Earlier, as a child, I had passed many a happy hour "helping out" on my Uncle Pete's "family" farm. But the area was also bisected by navigable rivers dotted with "mill towns"— small, poor communities dominated by THE MILL.

My family was inherently "cross-cultural." My dad was a last-minute escapee from Hungary under impending Nazi rule—other family members weren't so fortunate. He held a Ph.D. in chemical engineering but lacked English or money, so his first job in the US was farmhand. The expanding economy triggered by the war opened opportunities for him to (very successfully) pursue a career in his field. He was a very cultured man (as are/were all my paternal kin) who collected Rembrandt etchings and Ukiyo-e prints and loved the opera. My mother was the twelfth and last child of a family that had emigrated from Poland. They had been peasant farmers in Poland but became millworkers in the US. Their education was spotty and English pronunciation challenging. For three college summers, I labored in copper tubing and metal plating factories. This helped motivate me to earn the first college degree in the Sibole (my mother's) family, and escape the mill.

I had an idyllic childhood based on the ready availability of magnificent natural play spaces: the river that ran by the house (which was originally a tiny summer cottage), the nearby "woods," and plenty of green fields punctuated by perfect sledding hills. My experience of these wonders was mostly solo with occasional peer companionship, but never with parental oversight. I was "neglected" by my parents and it was wonderful. I played Little League for one season—my only pre-high-school encounter with organized extracurricular activity. My parents felt no necessity to watch me at play, let alone serve as my coach or cheerleader. I was also fortunate that my childhood was overshadowed by my parents' lingering memories of the Depression and the postwar scarcities. This meant that my "toys" and games were mostly improvised, invented, and self-made. I felt no sense of estrangement or resentment against my parents. On the contrary, I received a great deal of affection and the evening meal was definitely a "family" occasion to share our daily stories.

I was an ordinary kid with few noteworthy attributes. I had bad eyesight and was fascinated by babies and toddlers. Of course, no one guessed that this was a forecast of the future. After a brief detour to engineering (the apple did roll pretty far) I settled on psychology as my major, with a growing interest in the study of children's development. In a pure piece of serendipity, my supervisor in grad school had secured an NSF grant to do a comparative analysis of children's cognitive development in two sites—Costa Mesa, California and Sinyeé, Liberia—with just barely sufficient funds to send me to Liberia. As a research assistant I led middle-class American and tribal (Kpelle) fourth-graders through various problem-solving tasks, and recorded the results. There were certainly differences between the two groups, but the experimental results were neither very meaningful nor interesting. Yet, in the course of administering these tasks in Sinyeé, I started to note what was going on in the village and was struck by how different childhood was for a Kpelle village child and her counterpart from southern California.

I went back "into the field" to do my doctoral dissertation research, eventually published in 1996. My approach had changed to "ethnography" or "participant observation." Basically, I hunkered down in a remote Liberian village and watched/interacted with babies, children, and their older companions. Daily I recorded my observations and speculated on what it all meant. Within a short time after completing my degree, I was working on a multicultural and long-term research project in Papua New Guinea (PNG)—a living laboratory of human cultural variability. I tried to answer, with a comparative study that included nine contrasting cultures, some of the questions or conundrums that had remained after my Liberian research. To be honest, it took me many years to make much sense of my initial observations. My own research had to be augmented through my reading of the hundreds of accounts of childhood from all over the world and stretching very far back in time (e.g. children in ancient Egypt).

I also had the privilege, during the years in Papua New Guinea, to get to know children on a more sustained and intimate basis, namely my daughters Nadia and Sonia—the latter born in PNG. They taught me a great deal. The principle "finding" was the somewhat unwelcome message that parents have far less power to mold their offspring than they'd like. In fact I began our four-year residence in PNG with an experiment. The period—mid-1970s—was the height of the nature-versus-nurture debate with respect to gender. Scholar and lay adherents at both poles ("It's all nature." "It's all nurture.") were numerous. With a generous shipping allowance, we sent to our new home in PNG a varied array of toys and recreational props (e.g. easel, art supplies, Fisher-Price trucks, a construction set, wooden cars, various balls) and I constructed, soon after our arrival, a wooden jungle gym, sandbox, and tire swing. Conspicuously absent were any toys or props that might be considered exclusively or symbolically "girlie." According to the majority of authorities at the time, we would be materially aiding our daughters' education and employment opportunities by ensuring that they wouldn't be led into seeing themselves as the "lesser sex." I don't think either has ever suffered under that particular delusion but, nevertheless, their interest in the traditionally male toys and activities was conspicuously limited. Only when I joined in as a playmate did they engage with the trucks and road-building tools to erect a city in the sandbox. On the other hand, they raided the dirty-clothes basket and kitchen cupboards to assemble costumes and other props to act out self-scripted playlets in which they played distinctly feminine parts. The inspiration for this activity did not come from television or videos—we had none. They did not come from dolls and storybooks featuring demure, need-to-be-rescued females and heroic, gallant males—ditto. Their mother wore clothing, jewelry and makeup adapted to the hot, humid climate and "low" (contrasted with "high") society. But, in spite of my admonitions to the contrary, dolls etc. began, eventually, to arrive at our outpost, courtesy of grandparents. They were put into immediate and regular service and the limited interest in toy vehicles fell to naught.

By the end of my research in PNG and a post-doc at UCLA, I defined myself, academically, as a childhood anthropologist interested in studying the interaction of culture and biology in a child's development. Unfortunately, childhood anthropology did not exist as an academic category. No category, no jobs. So, for the next twelve years, I was employed but intellectually homeless until 1992 when I joined the Anthropology Faculty at Utah State University. A twelve-year hiatus from my chosen vocation wasn't erased overnight and it took quite a while to reboot. The critical motivating drive came from a growing sense of umbrage regarding the "export" of American (or, more specifically, WEIRD) ideas about children's play. Play advocates were promoting a model of play highlighting, in particular, a central role for parents as play instructors and coaches, and claiming that this was somehow essential, natural, and worthy of proselytization. I "knew" from my previous work on play in Liberian and Papua New Guinean villages, and the reports of anthropologists who'd observed play in villages around the world, that these claims about all children needing adult guidance and supervision were not only wrong but, in many ways, contradictory to the very nature of play. So I began a crusade-like endeavor to set the record straight. Now you have the "backstory" to the tale that began in Chapter 1.

Selected Sources

Chapter 1: Leave the Kids Alone

1. p. 1. H. Lukas and K. Hakami, "No baby talk: Children in a truly egalitarian society," *Hunter-Gatherer Research* (in press). Also K. Hakami, Anthropologist, University of Vienna, personal communication, 2015.
2. p. 2. D. F. Lancy, "'Playing with knives:' The socialization of self-initiated learners," *Child Development*, **87**, 2016.
3. p. 3. M. Erard, "The only baby book you'll ever need," *New York Times*, January 31, 2015.
4. p. 4. P. W. Turke, "Helpers at the nest: Childcare networks on Ifaluk." In L. Betzig, M. Borgerhoff Mulder, and P. Turke, eds., *Human Reproductive Behavior* (Cambridge: Cambridge University Press, 1988).
5. p. 4. O. Nieuwenhuys, "Growing up between places of work and non-places of childhood: The uneasy relationship." In K. F. Olwig and E. Gulløv, eds., *Children's Places: Cross-cultural Perspectives* (London: Routledge, 2003).
6. p. 6. D. F. Lancy, *The Anthropology of Childhood: Cherubs, Chattel, Changelings*, 2nd edition (Cambridge: Cambridge University Press, 2015).
7. p. 6. J. Henrich, S. J. Heine, and A. Norenzayan, "The weirdest people in the world?" *Behavioural and Brain Sciences*, **33**, 2010.
8. p. 8. King argues that mommy blogs may provide a modern substitute for the village model of learning to be a mother. W. L. King, "Mormon mommy blogs: 'There's gotta be some women out there who feel the same way'." Unpublished MS thesis. Utah State University, 2011.
9. p. 8. D. R. Regaignon, "Anxious uptakes: Nineteenth-century advice literature as a rhetorical genre," *College English*, **78**, 2015.

Chapter 2: Culture and Infancy

1. p. 9. C. Gallou, "Review of *The Anthropology of Childhood*," *Journal of Childhood in the Past*, **9**, 2016.
2. p. 9. A. Fisher, "Reproduction in Truk," *Ethnology*, **2**, 1963.

3. p. 10. R. Stasch, *Society of Others: Kinship and Mourning in a West Papuan Place* (Berkeley: University of California Press, 2009).

4. p. 10. M. Shostak, *Nisa: The Life and Words of a !Kung Woman* (New York: Vintage Books, 1981).

5. p. 10. P. Draper and E. Cashdan, "Technological change and child behavior among the !Kung," *Ethnology*, **27**, 1988.

6. p. 10. K. Hill and A. M. Hurtado, *Ache Life History: The Ecology and Demography of a Foraging People* (New York: Aldine de Gruyter, 1996).

Celebrating Babies

1. p. 12. D. A. Counts, "Infant care and feeding in Kaliai, West New Britain, Papua New Guinea." In L. B. Marshall, ed., *Infant Care and Feeding in the South Pacific* (New York: Gordon and Beach, 1985).

2. p. 12. J. Ritchie and J. Ritchie, *Growing Up in Polynesia* (Sydney: George Allen and Unwin, 1979).

3. p. 12. A. M. Tietjen, "Infant care and feeding practices and the beginnings of socialization among the Maisin of Papua New Guinea." In L. B. Marshall, ed., *Infant Care and Feeding in the South Pacific* (New York: Gordon and Beach, 1985).

4. p. 12. A. S. Wiley, *An Ecology of High-Altitude Infancy* (New York: Cambridge University Press, 2004).

5. pp. 12, 13. D. Kulick, *Language Shift and Cultural Reproduction: Socialization, Self, and Syncretism in a Papua New Guinea Village* (Cambridge: Cambridge University Press, 1992).

6. p. 13. D. B. McGilvray, "Sexual power and fertility in Sri Lanka: Batticaloa Tamils and Moors." In C. P. MacCormack, ed., *Ethnography of Fertility and Birth* (Prospect Heights, IL: Waveland Press, 1994).

7. p. 13. G. Gorer, *Himalayan Village: An Account of the Lepchas of Sikkim* (New York: Basic Books, 1967).

8. p. 13. M. Golden, *Children and Childhood in Classical Athens* (Baltimore, MD: Johns Hopkins University Press, 1990).

9. p. 13. M. Kleijueqgt, "Ancient Mediterranean world, childhood and adolescence." In R. A. Shweder, T. R. Bidell, A. C. Dailey, S. D. Dixon, P. J. Miller, and J. Modell, eds., *The Child: An Encyclopedic Companion* (Chicago: The University of Chicago Press, 2009).

10. p. 13. C. A. J. Little, "Becoming an Asabano: The socialization of Asabano children, Duranmin, West Sepik Province, Papua New

Guinea." Unpublished master's thesis. Trent University, Peterborough, Ontario, Canada, 2008.

11. p. 14. C. Wagley, *Welcome of Tears: The Tapirapé Indians of Central Brazil* (New York: Oxford University Press, 1977).

12. p. 14. S. B. Hrdy, *Mother Nature: Maternal Instincts and How They Shape the Human Species* (New York: Ballantine, 1999).

13. p. 14. K. A. Dettwyler, *Dancing Skeletons: Life and Death in West Africa* (Prospect Heights, IL: Waveland Press, 1972).

14. p. 14. J. Einarsdottir, *Tired of Weeping: Mother Love, Child Death, and Poverty in Guinea-Bissau* (Madison: The University of Wisconsin Press, 2004).

15. p. 15. D. R. Regaignon, "Anxious uptakes: Nineteenth-century advice literature as a rhetorical genre," *College English*, **78**, 2015.

16. p. 15. N. Scheper-Hughes, "Cultures, scarcity, and maternal thinking: Mother love and child death in Northeast Brazil." In N. Scheper-Hughes, ed., *Child Survival: Anthropological Perspectives on the Treatment and Maltreatment of Children* (Dordrecht: D. Reidel Publishing Company, 1987).

What about Swaddling?

1. p. 15. M. Mead, "The swaddling hypothesis: Its reception," *American Anthropologist*, **56**, 1954. In the same article, she discusses the role of swaddling in shaping "Russian character."

2. p. 16. P. Franco, N. Seret, J. N. Van Hees, S. Scaillet, J. Groswasser, and A. Kahn, "Influence of swaddling on sleep and arousal characteristics of healthy infants," *Pediatrics*, **115**, 2005.

3. p. 16. K. Calvert, *Children in the House: The Material Culture of Early Childhood, 1600–1900* (Boston: Northeastern University Press, 1992).

4. p. 16. M. J. Casimir, *Growing Up in a Pastoral Society: Socialization among Pashtu Nomads*, Kölner Ethnologische Beiträge (Cologne: Druck and Bindung, 2010).

5. p. 16. I. Fonseca, *Bury Me Standing: The Gypsies and Their Journey* (New York: Vintage Books, 1995).

6. p. 17. E. Z. Tronick, R. B. Thomas, and M. Daltabuit, "The Quechua manta pouch: A caretaking practice for buffering the Peruvian infant against the multiple stressors of high altitude," *Child Development*, **65**, 1994.

7. p. 17. M. A. MacKenzie, *Androgynous Objects: String Bags and Gender in Central New Guinea* (Reading: Harwood, 1991).

8. p. 17. J. S. Chisholm, "Development and adaptation in infancy," *New Directions for Child Development*, **8**, 1980.

9. p. 17. D. Leighton and C. C. Kluckhohn, *Children of the People* (Cambridge, MA: Harvard University Press, 1948).

10. p. 18. S. Harkness and C. Super, "Themes and variations: Parental ethnotheories in Western cultures." In K. H. Rubin and O. B. Chung, eds., *Parenting Beliefs, Behaviors, and Parent–Child Relations: A Cross-cultural Perspective* (New York: Psychology Press, 2006).

11. p. 18. H. Karp, *The Happiest Baby on the Block*, 2nd edition (New York: Bantam, 2015).

There Was an Old Woman . . .

1. p. 18. J. Ritson, *Gammer Gurton's Garland* (Whitefish, MT: Kessenger Reprint, 2009; first published 1794).

2. pp. 18, 19. J. Swift, *A Modest Proposal: For Preventing the Children of Poor People in Ireland, From Being a Burden on Their Parents or Country, and for Making Them Beneficial to the Publick* (Project Gutenberg, 1729). Available at www.gutenberg.org/catalog/world/readfile?fk_files=1444499.

3. p. 19. D. Kirka, "Albanian mom seeks to help family, but ends up losing son," *Salt Lake Tribune*, November 30, 2003.

4. p. 19. N. Scheper-Hughes, "Cultures, scarcity, and maternal thinking: Mother love and child death in Northeast Brazil." In N. Scheper-Hughes, ed., *Child Survival: Anthropological Perspectives on the Treatment and Maltreatment of Children* (Dordrecht: D. Reidel Publishing Company, 1987).

5. pp. 19, 20. J. Einarsdottir, *Tired of Weeping: Mother Love, Child Death, and Poverty in Guinea-Bissau* (Madison: The University of Wisconsin Press, 2004).

6. p. 20. K. Hampshire, "The impact of male migration on fertility decisions and outcomes in northern Burkina Faso." In S. Tremayne, ed., *Managing Reproductive Life: Cross-cultural Themes in Sexuality and Fertility* (Oxford: Berghahn Books, 2001).

7. p. 20. M. Konner and C. Worthman, "Nursing frequency, gonadal function and birth spacing among !Kung hunter-gatherers," *Science*, **207**, 1980.

8. p. 20. B. M. Gray, "Enga birth, maturation and survival: Physiological characteristics of the life cycle in the New Guinea Highlands." In C. P. MacCormack, ed., *Ethnography of Fertility and Birth* (Prospect Heights, IL: Waveland Press, 1994).

9. p. 20. L. E. Belaunde, "Menstruation, birth observances and the couple's love amongst the Airo-Pai of Amazonian Peru." In S. Tremayne, ed., *Managing Reproductive Life: Cross-cultural Themes in Sexuality and Fertility* (Oxford: Berghahn Books, 2001).

10. p. 20. B. S. Hewlett, "Demography and childcare in preindustrial societies," *Journal of Anthropological Research*, **47**, 1991.

11. p. 21. D. Alexandre-Bidon and D. Lett, *Children in the Middle Ages: Fifth–Fifteen Centuries* (Notre Dame, IN: The University of Notre Dame Press, 1999).

12. p. 21. J. C. Sommerville, *The Rise and Fall of Childhood* (Beverly Hills, CA: Sage Publications, 1982).

13. p. 21. P. Gavitt, *Charity and Children in Renaissance Florence: The Ospedale degli Innocenti, 1410–1536* (Ann Arbor: The University of Michigan Press, 1990).

14. p. 22. A. R. Colón with P. A. Colón, *A History of Children: A Socio-cultural Survey across Millennia* (Westport, CT: Greenwood Press, 2001).

15. p. 22. Sommerville, *The Rise and Fall of Childhood*.

16. p. 22. S. R. Johansson, "Neglect, abuse, and avoidable death: Parental investment and the mortality of infants and children in the European tradition." In R. J. Gelles and J. B. Lancaster, eds., *Child Abuse and Neglect: Biosocial Dimensions* (New York: Aldine de Gruyter, 1976).

17. p. 22. Sommerville, *The Rise and Fall of Childhood*.

18. p. 22. N. Chaudhuri, "England." In J. M. Hawes and N. R. Hiner, eds., *Children in Historical and Comparative Perspective* (Westport, CT: Greenwood Press, 1991).

19. p. 22. Sommerville, *The Rise and Fall of Childhood*.

20. p. 22. B. Moynihan, *The Faith: A History of Christianity* (New York: Doubleday, 2002).

21. p. 22. S. Mintz, *Huck's Raft: A History of American Childhood* (Cambridge, MA: Belknap Press, 2004).

22. p. 23. J. C. Caldwell, *"The Great Transition": Theory of Fertility Decline* (New York: Academic Press, 1982).

23. p. 23. D. F. Lancy, *The Anthropology of Childhood: Cherubs, Chattel, Changelings*, 2nd edition (Cambridge: Cambridge University Press, 2015).

24. p. 23. D. W. Lawson and R. Mace, "Optimizing modern family size," *Human Nature*, **21**, 2010.

25. p. 23. V. A. Zelizer, *Pricing the Priceless Child: The Changing Social Value of Children* (New York: Basic Books, 1985).

26. p. 23. http://inashoe.com.

27. p. 23. W. M. Hern, "Family planning, Amazon style," *Natural History*, **101**(12), 1992.

28. p. 23. K. W. Terhune, "A review of the actual and expected consequences of family size," *Calspan Report*, DP-5333-G-1 (Washington, DC: Center for Population Research, National Institute of Child Health and Human Development, 1974).

29. p. 23. J. Blake, *Family Size and Achievement* (Berkeley: University of California Press, 1989).

30. p. 24. D. W. Lawson and R. Mace, "Trade-offs in modern parenting: A longitudinal study of sibling competition for parental care," *Human Behavior*, **30**(3), 2009.

31. p. 24. B. P. Zhu, "Effect of inter-pregnancy interval on birth outcomes: findings from three recent US studies," *International Journal of Gynecology and Obstetrics*, **89**, 2005.

Chapter 3: Questions about Infant Attachment

1. p. 25. L. M. Steiner, *Mommy Wars: Stay-at-Home and Career Moms Face Off on Their Choices, Their Lives, Their Families* (New York: Random House, 2007).

2. p. 25. J. Bowlby, *Child Care and The Growth of Love* (Hammondsworth: Penguin, 1961).

3. p. 25. M. D. Salter Ainsworth, M. C. Blehar, E. Waters, and S. N. Wall, *Patterns of Attachment: A Psychological Study of the Strange Situation* (Hillsdale, NJ: Erlbaum, 1978).

4. p. 25. http://www.attachmentparenting.org.

5. p. 25. http://www.attachment.org.

6. p. 26. http://online.wsj.com/article/SB10001424052748704462704575590603553674296.html?KEYWORDS=erica+jong.

7. p. 26. E. Jenner, "The perils of attachment parenting," *Atlantic Magazine*, August 2014.

8. p. 26. H. Otto and H. Keller, eds., *Different Faces of Attachment: Cultural Variations of a Universal Human Need* (Cambridge: Cambridge University Press, 2014).

N. Quinn and J. Mageo, eds., *Attachment Reconsidered: Cultural Perspectives on a Western Theory* (New York: Palgrave-Macmillan, 2013).

9. p. 26. G. M. Erchak, *The Anthropology of Self and Behavior* (New Brunswick, NJ: Rutgers University Press, 1992).

10. p. 27. R. Paradise, "Passivity or tacit collaboration: Mazahua interaction in cultural context," *Learning and Instruction*, **6**, 1996.

11. p. 27. R. A. LeVine, "Challenging expert knowledge: Findings from an African study of infant care and development." In U. P. Gielen and J. L. Roopnarine, eds., *Childhood and Adolescence: Cross-cultural Perspectives and Application* (Westport, CT: Praeger, 2004).

12. p. 27. B. Sandlin, "Children and the Swedish welfare state: From different to familiar." In P. S. Fass and G. Michael, eds., *Reinventing Childhood after World War II* (Philadelphia: University of Pennsylvania Press, 2012).

13. p. 27. R. LeVine and K. Norman, "The infant's acquisition of culture: Early attachment reexamined in anthropological perspective." In C. C. Moore and H. F. Matthews, eds., *The Psychology of Cultural Experience* (Cambridge: Cambridge University Press, 2001).

Detachment Parenting

1. p. 28. D. F. Lancy, "Babies aren't persons." In H. Keller and H. Otto, eds., *Different Faces of Attachment: Cultural Variations of a Universal Human Need* (Cambridge: Cambridge University Press, 2014).

2. p. 28. C. Heywood, *A History of Childhood: Children and Childhood in the West from Medieval to Modern Times* (Cambridge: Polity Press, 2001).

3. p. 29. Ibid.

4. pp. 29, 30. A. S. Wiley, *An Ecology of High-Altitude Infancy* (Cambridge: Cambridge University Press, 2004).

5. p. 30. M. Tomlinson, L. Murray, and P. Cooper, "Attachment theory, culture, and Africa: Past, present, and future." In P. Erdmand and K. Ng, eds., *Attachment: Expanding the Cultural Connections* (New York: Routledge, 2010).

6. p. 31. J. Einarsdottir, *Tired of Weeping: Mother Love, Child Death, and Poverty in Guinea-Bissau* (Madison: The University of Wisconsin Press, 2004).

7. pp. 30, 31, 32. Lancy, "Babies aren't persons."

8. p. 32. Ibid.

9. p. 32. J. E. Grubbs, "Infant exposure and infanticide." In J. E. Grubbs, T. Parkin, and R. Bell, eds., *The Oxford Handbook of Childhood and Education in the Classical World* (Oxford: Oxford University Press, 2013).

10. p. 32. V. A. Zelizer, *Pricing the Priceless Child: The Changing Social Value of Children* (New York: Basic Books, 1985).

11. p. 33. D. Alexandre-Bidon and D. Lett, *Children in the Middle Ages: Fifth–Fifteen Centuries* (Notre Dame, IN: The University of Notre Dame Press, 1999).

Babies Aren't People

1. pp. 33–7. D. F. Lancy, "Babies aren't persons." In H. Keller and H. Otto, eds., *Different Faces of Attachment: Cultural Variations of a Universal Human Need* (Cambridge: Cambridge University Press, 2014).

2. p. 34. S. Harkness, C. M. Super, and C. H. Keefer, "Learning to be an American parent: How cultural models gain directive force." In R. D'Andrade and C. Strauss, eds., *Human Motives and Cultural Models* (Cambridge: Cambridge University Press, 1992).

3. p. 35. R. D. Whittemore, "Child caregiving and socialization to the Mandinka way: Toward an ethnography of childhood." Unpublished Ph.D. dissertation. University of California, Los Angeles, 1989.

4. p. 35. G. M. Childs, *Umbundu Kinship and Character: Being a Description of Social Structure and Individual Development of the Ovimbundu of Angola* (London: Published for the International African Institute by the Oxford University Press, 1949).

5. p. 36. C.-É. de Suremain, "Au fil de la faja: Enrouler et dérouler la vie en Bolivie." In D. Bonnet and L. Pourchez, eds., *Du soin au rite dans l'infance* (Paris: IRD, 2007).

6. p. 37. B. Rawson, *Children and Childhood in Roman Italy* (Oxford: Oxford University Press, 2003).

7. p. 37. M. E. Lewis, *The Bioarchaeology of Children: Perspectives from Biological and Forensic Anthropology* (Cambridge: Cambridge University Press, 2007).

8. p. 38. D. F. Lancy, *The Anthropology of Childhood: Cherubs, Chattel, Changelings*, 2nd edition (Cambridge: Cambridge University Press, 2015).

9. p. 38. G. Cross, *The Cute and the Cool: Wondrous Innocence and Modern American Children's Culture* (New York: Oxford University Press, 2004).

Devils or Angels?

1. p. 39. A. Dupuis, "Rites requis par la naissance, la croissance et la mort des jumeaux: Leur aménagement dans le monde modern. Le cas de Nzebi du Gabon." In D. Bonnet and L. Pourchez, eds., *Du soin au rite dans l'infance* (Paris: IRD, 2007).
2. p. 39. C.-É. de Suremain, "Au fil de la faja: Enrouler et dérouler la vie en Bolivie." In D. Bonnet and L. Pourchez, eds., *Du soin au rite dans l'infance* (Paris: IRD, 2007).
3. pp. 39, 40, 41, 42. D. F. Lancy, *The Anthropology of Childhood: Cherubs, Chattel, Changelings*, 2nd edition (Cambridge: Cambridge University Press, 2015).
4. p. 40. E. Scott, *The Archaeology of Infancy and Infant Death* (Oxford: Archaeopress, 1999).
5. p. 40. John D. Viccars, "Witchcraft in Bolobo, Belgian Congo," *Africa: Journal of the International African Institute*, **19**(3), 1949.
6. p. 41. K. Tjitayi and S. Lewis, "Envisioning lives at Ernabella." In U. Eickelkamp, ed., *Growing Up in Central Australia: New Anthropological Studies of Aboriginal Childhood and Adolescence* (Oxford: Berghahn Books, 2011).
7. p. 41. Y. V. S. Nath, *Bhils of Ratanmal: An Analysis of the Social Structure of a Western Indian Community*, The M.S. University Sociological Monograph Series I (Baroda: Maharaja Sayajirao University of Baroda, 1960).
8. p. 43. G. Cross, *The Cute and the Cool: Wondrous Innocence and Modern American Children's Culture* (New York: Oxford University Press, 2004).

"Baby-Parading": Childcare or Showing Off?

1. p. 43. www.fatherhoodinstitute.org/2014/fi-research-summary-fathers-and-attachment.
2. pp. 43, 44. B. S. Hewlett, *Intimate Fathers: The Nature and Context of Aka Pygmy Paternal–Infant Care* (Ann Arbor: University of Michigan Press, 1991).

3. p. 44. D. F. Lancy, *The Anthropology of Childhood: Cherubs, Chattel, Changelings*, 2nd edition (Cambridge: Cambridge University Press, 2015).

4. p. 44. C. Hua, *A Society without Fathers or Husbands: The Na of China* (Asti Husvedt, translator) (Brooklyn, NY: Zone Books, 2001).

5. p. 44. D. W. Gegeo and K. A. Watson-Gegeo, "Kwara'ae mothers and infants: Changing family practices." In L. B. Marshall, ed., *Infant Care and Feeding in the South Pacific: Health, Work, and Childrearing* (New York: Gordon and Beach Science, 1985).

6. p. 44. B. M. Gray, "Enga birth, maturation and survival: Physiological characteristics of the life cycle in the New Guinea Highlands." In C. P. MacCormack, ed., *Ethnography of Fertility and Birth* (Prospect Heights, IL: Waveland Press, 1994).

7. p. 44. J. Bock and S. E. Johnson, "Male migration, remittances, and child outcome among the Okavango Delta peoples of Botswana." In C. S. Tamis-LaMonda and N. Cabrera, eds., *Handbook of Father Involvement: Multidisciplinary Perspectives* (Mahwah, NJ: Erlbaum, 2002).

8. p. 45. R. Sear and R. Mace, "Who keeps children alive? A review of the effects of kin on child survival," *Evolution and Human Behavior*, **29**, 2008.

9. p. 46. B. Welles-Nyström, "Scenes from a marriage: Equality ideology in Swedish family policy, maternal ethnotheories, and practice." In S. Harkness and C. M. Super, eds., *Parents' Cultural Belief Systems: Their Origins, Expressions, and Consequences* (New York: The Guilford Press, 1996).

10. p. 46. M. Jolivet, *Japan: The Childless Society? The Crisis of Motherhood* (London: Routledge, 1997).

11. p. 46. C. C. Miller, "Men do more at home, but not as much as they think," *New York Times*, November 12, 2015.

12. p. 46. R. La Rossa, "Fatherhood and social change," *Family Relations*, **37**, 1988.

13. p. 47. J. D. Berrick, *Faces of Poverty: Portraits of Women and Children on Welfare* (New York: Oxford University Press, 1995).

14. p. 47. F. Galindo ("Feggo"), cartoon, *New Yorker*, September 19, 2005.

15. p. 47. G. L. Brase, "Cues of parental investment as a factor in attractiveness," *Evolution and Human Behavior*, **27**, 2006.

16. p. 47. J. Pleck, "American fathering in historical perspective." In M. S. Kimmel, ed., *Changing Men: New Directions in Research on Men and Masculinity* (Beverly Hills, CA: Sage Publications, 1987).

Chapter 4: Children Playing and Learning

1. p. 48. H. B. Schwartzman, *Transformations: The Anthropology of Children's Play* (New York: Plenum, 1978).
2. p. 48. J. M. Roberts and B. Sutton-Smith, "Child training and game involvement," *Ethnology*, **2**, 1962.
3. p. 48. D. F. Lancy, "Play in species adaptation." In B. J. Siegel, ed., *Annual Review of Anthropology*, **9**, 1980.

Cowboys and Indians and the Origin of the Couch Potato

1. pp. 49, 50. D. F. Lancy, *Playing on the Mother-Ground: Cultural Routines for Children's Development* (New York: Guilford, 1996).
2. p. 50. F. De Laguna, "Childhood among the Yakutat Tlingit." In M. E. Spiro, ed., *Context and Meaning in Cultural Anthropology* (New York: Free Press, 1965).
3. p. 50. M. Fortes, "Social and psychological aspects of education in Taleland." In J. Middleton, ed., *From Child to Adult: Studies in the Anthropology of Education* (Garden City, NY: The Natural History Press, 1938/1970).
4. p. 50. B. Spencer and F. Gillen, *The Arunta: A Study of a Stone Age People* (London: Macmillan, 1927).
5. p. 51. P. McClaren, *Cries from the Corridor* (Toronto, ON: Methuen, 1980).
6. p. 51. D. F. Lancy and B. L. Hayes, "Interactive fiction and the reluctant reader," *English Journal*, **77**(6), 1988.
7. p. 52. N. Barber, "Play and regulation in mammals," *Quarterly Review of Biology*, **66**, 1991.
8. p. 52. L. Sax, *Boys Adrift: The Five Factors Driving the Growing Epidemic of Unmotivated Boys and Underachieving Young Men* (New York: Basic, 2007).
9. p. 52. The American Academy of Pediatrics website provides documentation of the deleterious effects of excessive engagement with electronic media and provides strategies to reduce "screen time." See http://search.aap.org/?source=aap.org&k=screen%20time&AspxA utoDetectCookieSupport=1.
10. p. 53. J. E. Arnold, "Mountains of things." In E. Ochs and T. Kremer-Sadlik, eds., *Fast-Forward Families: Home, Work, and*

Relationships in Middle-Class America (Berkeley: University of California Press, 2013).

11. p. 53. C. A. Anderson, A. Craig, Akiko Shibuya, Nobuko Ihori, and Muniba Saleem, "Violent video game effects on aggression, empathy, and prosocial behavior in Eastern and Western countries: A meta-analytic review." *Psychological Bulletin*, **136**, 2010.

12. p. 53. In the first three months of 2016, fifty-seven children in the USA used a gun to harm or kill someone.

Toys or Tools?

1. p. 53. B. Dawe, "Tiny arrowheads: Toys in the toolkit," *Plains Anthropology*, **42**, 1997.

2. p. 54. F. Boas, "The Eskimo of Baffin Land and Hudson Bay," *Bulletin of the American Museum of Natural History*, **15**, Part 1, 1901.

3. p. 54. D. Jenness, *The Life of the Copper Eskimos.* Report of the Canadian Arctic Expedition, **12**(A), Ottawa, Canada, 1922.

4. p. 54. B. J. Bowser and J. Q. Patton, "Learning and transmission of pottery style: Women's life histories and communities of practice in the Ecuadorian Amazon." In M. T. Stark, B. J. Bowser, and L. Horne, eds., *Breaking Down Boundaries: Anthropological Approaches to Cultural Transmission, Learning, and Material Culture* (Tucson: University of Arizona Press, 2008).

5. p. 54. M. M. Edel, *The Chiga of Uganda*, 2nd edition (New Brunswick, NJ: Transaction Publishers, 1957/1996).

6. pp. 54, 55. D. F. Lancy, "'Playing with knives': The socialization of self-initiated learners," *Child Development*, **87**, 2016.

7. p. 55. E. Bonawitz, P. Shafto, H. Gweon, and L. Schulz, "The double-edged sword of pedagogy: Instruction limits spontaneous exploration and discovery," *Cognition*, **120**, 2011.

8. p. 55. C. Dyer and A. Choksi, "With God's grace and with education, we will find a way: Literacy, education, and the Rabaris of Kutch, India." In C. Dyer, ed., *The Education of Nomadic Peoples: Current Issues, Future Prospects* (Oxford: Berghahn Books, 2006).

9. p. 57. C. Gross–Loh, *Parenting without Borders* (New York: Avery, 2013).

10. p. 58. K. J. Pine and A. Nash, "Dear Santa: The effects of television advertising on young children," *International Journal of Behavioral Development*, **26**(6), 2002.

11. p. 58. A. J. Clarke, "Coming of age in suburbia: Gifting the consumer child." In M. Gutman and N. de Coninck-Smith, eds., *Designing Modern Childhoods: History, Space, and the Material Culture of Children* (New Brunswick, NJ: Rutgers University Press, 2008).
12. p. 58. E. Clark, *The Real Toy Story: Inside the Ruthless Battle for America's Youngest Consumers* (New York: Free Press, 2007).
13. p. 58. M. H. MacElroy, *Work and Play in Colonial Days* (New York: MacMillan, 1917).
14. p. 58. G. Cross, *Kid's Stuff: Toys and the Changing World of American Childhood* (Cambridge, MA: Harvard University Press, 1999).

Gamesmanship

1. p. 59. J. Piaget, *The Moral Judgment of the Child* (Marjorie Gabain, translator) (New York: Free Press, 1932/1965).
2. p. 60. D. F. Lancy, *The Anthropology of Childhood: Cherubs, Chattel, Changelings*, 2nd edition (Cambridge: Cambridge University Press, 2015).
3. p. 60. I. Opie and P. Opie, *Children's Games with Things* (Oxford: Oxford University Press, 1997).
4. p. 60. Piaget, *The Moral Judgment of the Child*.
5. p. 61. Ibid.
6. p. 61. Ibid.
7. p. 61. H. B. Schwartzman, *Transformations: The Anthropology of Children's Play* (New York: Plenum, 1978).
8. p. 61. S. Gaskins, W. Haight, and D. F. Lancy, "The cultural construction of play." In A. Göncü and S. Gaskins, eds., *Play and Development: Evolutionary, Sociocultural, and Functional Perspectives* (Mahwah, NJ: Erlbaum, 2007).
9. p. 62. B. Smith, "Of marbles and (little) men: Bad luck and masculine identification in Aymara boyhood," *Journal of Linguistic Anthropology*, **20**, 2010.
10. p. 62. Lancy, *The Anthropology of Childhood*.
11. p. 62. M. H. Goodwin, *The Hidden Life of Girls: Games of Stance, Status, and Exclusion* (Malden, MA: Blackwell Publishing, 2006).
12. p. 62. H. I. Hogbin, "A New Guinea childhood: From weaning till the eighth year in Wogeo," *Oceania*, **16**, 1946.
13. p. 62. K. O. Burridge, "A Tangu game," *Man*, **57**, 1957.

14. pp. 62, 63. P. Draper, "Social and economic constraints on child life among the !Kung." In R. B. Lee and I. DeVore, eds., *Kalahari Hunter-Gatherers: Studies of the !Kung San and Their Neighbors* (Cambridge, MA: Harvard University Press, 1976).

15. p. 63. A. H. Boyette, "Children's play and culture learning in an egalitarian forager society," *Child Development,* **87,** 2016.

16. p. 63. I. Opie and P. Opie, *Children's Games in Street and Playground* (Oxford: Clarendon Press, 1969).

17. p. 63. R. Byrne, *The Thinking Ape* (Oxford: Oxford University Press 1995).

18. p. 63. D. F. Lancy and M. A. Grove, "Marbles and Machiavelli: The role of game play in children's social development," *American Journal of Play,* **3,** 2011.

19. pp. 63, 64. G. A. Fine, *With the Boys: Little League Baseball and Preadolescent Culture* (Chicago: The University of Chicago Press, 1987).

20. p. 65. Gaskins, Haight, and Lancy, "The cultural construction of play."

21. p. 65. H. E. Marano, *A Nation of Wimps* (New York: Broadway Books, 2008).

22. p. 65. R. A. Marcom, "Moving up the grades: Relationship between preschool model and later school success." *Early Childhood Research and Practice,* **4**(1), 2002.

23. p. 65. W. Hu, "Forget goofing around: Recess has a new boss," *New York Times,* March 15, 2010. Available at http://www.nytimes.com/ 2010/03/15/education/15recess.html.

24. p. 65. L. Skenazy, *Free-Range Kids: Giving Our Children the Freedom We Had Without Going Nuts with Worry* (Danvers, MA: Jossey–Bass, 2009).

25. p. 65. Horsham Primary School, "Marbles at Horsham Primary School," *Play and Folklore,* **54,** 2010.

Chapter 5: Protection versus Suppression

1. p. 66. F. Furedi, *Paranoid Parenting: Why Ignoring the Experts May Be Best for Your Child* (Chicago: Chicago Review Press, 2002).

2. pp. 66, 67, 68. E. B. H. Sandsetter and O. J. Sando, "'We don't allow children to climb trees': How a focus on safety affects Norwegian

children's play in early-childhood education and care settings," *American Journal of Play*, **8**, 2016.

3. p. 68. J. Bristow, "The double bind of parenting culture: Helicopter parents and cotton wool kids." In E. Lee, J. Bristow, C. Faircloth, and J. Macvarish, *Parenting Culture Studies* (Basingstoke: Palgrave Macmillan, 2014).

4. p. 68. J. Qvortrup, "Varieties of childhood." In J. Qvortrup, ed., *Studies in Modern Childhood: Society, Agency, Culture* (Basingstoke: Palgrave, 2005).

5. p. 68. E. Seiter, "Children's desires/mothers' dilemmas: The social contexts of consumption." In H. Jenkins, ed., *The Children's Culture Reader* (New York: New York University Press, 1998).

6. p. 68. A. J. Clarke, "Coming of age in suburbia: Gifting the consumer child." In M. Gutman and N. de Coninck-Smith, eds., *Designing Modern Childhoods: History, Space, and the Material Culture of Children* (New Brunswick, NJ: Rutgers University Press, 2008).

7. p. 68. P. K. Smith, *Children and Play* (Chichester: Wiley-Blackwell, 2010).

8. pp. 68, 69. A. Curry, "The unintended (and deadly) consequences of living in the industrialized world," *Smithsonian Magazine*, April 2013.

9. p. 69. M. Holbreich, J. Genuneit, J. Weber, and E. von Mutius, "Amish children living in northern Indiana have a very low prevalence of allergic sensitization," *Journal of Allergy and Clinical Immunology*, **129**, 2012.

10. p. 69. Curry, "The unintended (and deadly) consequences of living in the industrialized world."

11. pp. 69, 70. Roy F. Baumeister, J. D. Campbell, J. I. Krueger, and K. D. Vohs, "Exploding the self-esteem myth," *Scientific American Mind*, **16**(4), 2005.

12. p. 70. D. E. Beals, "Eating and reading: Links between family conversations with preschoolers and later language and literacy." In D. K. Dickinson and P. O. Tabors, eds., *Beginning Literacy with Language* (Baltimore, MD: Paul H. Brooks, 2001).

13. p. 70. S. Kawash, "Gangsters, pranksters and the invention of trick-or-treating, 1930–1960," *American Journal of Play*, **4**, 2011.

14. p. 70. L. Skenazy, "'Stranger danger' and the decline of Halloween: No child has ever been killed by poisoned candy. Ever," *Wall Street*

Journal, October 27, 2010. Available at http://online.wsj.com/article/ SB10001424052702304915104575572642896563902.html?mod=WS J_hpp_sections_opinion.

15. p. 70. C. D. Clark, "Tricks of festival: Children, enculturation, and American Halloween," *Ethos*, **33**, 2005.
16. p. 70. A. J. Pugh, *Longing and Belonging: Parents, Children, and Consumer Culture* (Berkeley: University of California Press, 2009).
17. p. 70. P. S. Fass, "Abduction stories that changed our lives: From Charley Ross to modern behavior." In P. N. Stearns, ed., *American Behavioral History: An Introduction* (New York: New York University Press, 2005).
18. p. 70. H. E. Marano, *A Nation of Wimps* (New York: Broadway Books, 2008).
19. p. 70. G. Cross, *The Cute and the Cool: Wondrous Innocence and Modern American Children's Culture* (New York: Oxford University Press, 2004).
20. pp. 70, 71. J. Zimmerman, *Whose America? Culture Wars in the Public Schools* (Cambridge, MA: Harvard University Press, 2002).
21. p. 72. S. Chanthavong, *Chocolate and Slavery: Child Labor in Côte d'Ivoire*, TED Case Studies # 664, 2002. Available at www1.ameri can.edu/ted/chocolate-slave.htm.

Nanny Angst

1. p. 72. B. K. Packer, "For time and all eternity," *Ensign*, November 1993.
2. p. 73. J. Brooks-Gunn, W. Han, and J. Waldfogel, "First-year maternal employment and child development in the first 7 years," *Monographs of the Society for Research in Child Development*, **75**(2), 2010.
3. p. 73. D. Durham, "Apathy and agency: The romance of agency and youth in Botswana." In J. Cole and D. Durham, eds., *Figuring the Future: Globalism and the Temporalities of Children and Youth* (Santa Fe: School for Advanced Research Press, 2008).
4. p. 73. K. Hawkes, J. F. O'Connell, N. G. Blurton Jones, H. Alvarez, and E. L. Charnov, "The grandmother hypothesis and human evolution." In L. Cronk, N. Chagnon, and W. Irons, eds., *Adaptation and Human Behavior: An Anthropological Perspective* (Hawthorne, NY: Aldine de Gruyter, 2000).
5. p. 73. T. S. Weisner and R. Gallimore, "My brother's keeper: Child and sibling caretaking," *Current Anthropology*, **18**(2), 1977.

6. p. 73. H. R. Clinton, *It Takes a Village* (New York: Simon and Schuster, 1996).

7. p. 74. B. S. Hewlett, *Intimate Fathers: The Nature and Context of Aka Pygmy Paternal–Infant Care* (Ann Arbor: University of Michigan Press, 1991).

8. p. 75. J. C. Sommerville, *The Rise and Fall of Childhood* (Beverly Hills, CA: Sage Publications, 1982).

9. p. 75. K. R. Bradley, *Discovering the Roman Family: Studies in Roman Social History* (Oxford: Oxford University Press, 1991).

10. p. 75. G. Dahlberg, "The parent–child relationship and socialization in the context of modern childhood: The case of Sweden." In J. L. Roopnarine and D. B. Carter, eds., *Parent–Child Socialization in Diverse Cultures* (Norwood, NJ: Ablex Publishing Corporation, 1992).

Child-Proofing versus Tool Using

1. p. 76. S. J. Shennan and J. Steele, "Cultural learning in hominids: A behavioral ecological approach." In H. O. Box and K. R. Gibson, eds., *Mammalian Social Learning: Comparative and Ecological Perspectives* (Cambridge: Cambridge University Press, 1999).

2. p. 77. K. Connolly and M. Dalgleish, "The emergence of tool-using skill in infancy," *Developmental Psychology*, **25**, 1989. A parallel study, with similar results, involved monitoring the toddler's gradual mastery of using a hammer to drive a peg into a board. Again, the appropriate motor movements emerge with increasing age and practice but absent any "instruction."

3. pp. 78, 79, 80. D. F. Lancy, "'Playing with knives:' The socialization of self-initiated learners," *Child Development*, **87**, 2016.

4. p. 80. C. Gross–Loh, *Parenting without Borders* (New York: Avery, 2013).

5. p. 81. W. Klein and M. H. Goodwin, "Chores." In E. Ochs and T. Kremer-Sadlik, eds., *Fast-Forward Families: Home, Work, and Relationships* (Berkeley: University of California Press, 2013).

What Price Happiness?

1. p. 81. A. J. Pugh, *Longing and Belonging: Parents, Children, and Consumer Culture* (Berkeley: University of California Press, 2009).

2. pp. 81, 82. M. Dale, "Mom of boy who planned school shooting arrested," *Salt Lake Tribune*, October 13, 2007.

3. p. 82. H. Montgomery, *Modern Babylon: Prostituting Children in Thailand* (Oxford: Berghahn Books, 2001).

4. p. 82. C. A. Lutz, *Unnatural Emotions: Everyday Sentiments on a Micronesian Atoll and Their Challenge to Western Theory* (Chicago: The University of Chicago Press, 1988).

5. p. 82. F. W. Marlowe, *The Hadza: Hunter-Gatherers of Tanzania* (Berkeley: University of California Press, 2010).

6. p. 82. H. Cunningham, *Children and Childhood in Western Society since 1500* (New York: Longman, 1995).

7. p. 82. E. Langmuir, *Imagining Childhood* (New Haven, CT: Yale University Press, 2006).

8. pp. 82, 83. P. N. Stearns, "Defining happy childhoods: Assessing a recent change," *Journal of the History of Childhood and Youth*, **3**, 2010.

9. p. 83. D. J. Walsh, "Frog boy and the American monkey: The body in Japanese early schooling." In L. Bresler, ed., *Knowing Bodies, Moving Minds* (Dordrecht: Kluwer Academic Publishers, 2004). See also M.-L. Hopgood, *How Eskimos Keep Their Babies Warm: And Other Adventures in Parenting* (Chapel Hill, NC: Algonquin Books, 2012).

10. p. 84. R. Wiseman, *Queen Bees and Wannabes: Helping Your Daughter Survive Cliques, Gossip, Boyfriends, and Other Realities of Adolescence* (New York: Three Rivers Press, 2003).

11. p. 84. A. Robbins, *The Overachievers: The Secret Lives of Driven Kids* (New York: Hyperion, 2006).

12. p. 84. A. Chua, *Battle Hymn of the Tiger Mother* (New York: Penguin Press, 2011).

13. p. 84. L. S. Merriman, "It's your child's education, not yours," *Chronicle of Higher Education*, November 23, 2007.

14. p. 84. R. F. Baumeister, J. D. Campbell, J. I. Krueger, and K. D. Vohs, "Exploding the self-esteem myth," *Scientific American Mind*, **16**(4), 2005.

Turning Inside Out *Inside Out*

1. p. 86. J. Henrich, S. J. Heine, and A. Norenzayan, "The weirdest people in the world?", *Behavioural and Brain Sciences*, **33**, 2010.

2. p. 86. D. F. Lancy, *The Anthropology of Childhood: Cherubs, Chattel, Changelings*, 2nd edition (Cambridge: Cambridge University Press, 2015).

3. p. 86. S. Firestone, *The Dialectic of Sex: The Case for Feminist Revolution* (London: Jonathan Cape, 1971).

4. pp. 86, 87. F. Furedi, *Therapy Culture: Cultivating Vulnerability in an Uncertain Age* (London: Routledge, 2004).

5. p. 87. J. M. Zito, D. J. Safer, S. DosReis, J. F. Gardner, L. Magder, K. Soeken, M. Boles, F. Lynch, and M. A. Riddle, "Psychotropic practice patterns in youth," *Archives of Pediatrics and Adolescent Medicine*, **157**, 2003.

6. p. 88. R. Wiseman, *Queen Bees and Wannabes: Helping Your Daughter Survive Cliques, Gossip, Boyfriends, and Other Realities of Adolescence* (New York: Three Rivers Press, 2003).

7. p. 88. http://disney.wikia.com/wiki/Inside_Out.

Chapter 6: Going to School

1. p. 90. http://www.snowboardinghelp.com/using-lifts/poma-lifts-the-pogo-sticks-of-the-ski-hills.php.

2. p. 91. A. Gopnik, *The Gardener and the Carpenter: What the New Science of Child Development Tells Us about the Relationship between Parents and Children* (New York: Farrar, Straus and Giroux, 2016).

3. pp. 91, 92. L. Acredolo and S. Goodwyn, *Baby Signs: How to Talk with Your Baby Before Your Baby Can Talk* (Chicago: Contemporary Books, 2002).

The Resistant Scholar: Don't Blame Teachers, Schools, Curricula, or Television

1. p. 93. ACT 2014. The Condition of College and Career Readiness—2014. Iowa City: American College Testing Service, at http://www.act.org/content/act/en/research/condition-of-college-and-career-readiness-report-2014.html?page=0&chapter=0.

2. pp. 93, 94. C. Morelli, "Learning to sit still: The physical implications of schooling for Matses children in the Peruvian Amazon." Paper

presented at a workshop, Schooling in Anthropology: Learning the "Modern Way," Brunel University, December 5, 2011.

3. p. 94. A. Stambach, "'Too much studying makes me crazy:' School-related illnesses on Mount Kilimanjaro," *Comparative Education Review*, **42**, 1998.

4. p. 94. G. Spittler, "Children's work in a family economy: A case study and theoretical discussion." In G. Spittler and M. Bourdillon, eds., *African Children at Work: Working and Learning in Growing Up* (Berlin: LIT Verlag, 2012).

5. p. 94. L. Gilliam, "Calm children, wild children: Exploring the relation between civilizing projects and children's school identities." Paper presented at American Anthropological Association Annual Meeting, San Francisco, November 2008.

6. p. 94. M. F. Durantini, *The Child in Seventeenth-Century Dutch Painting* (Ann Arbor, MI: UMI Research Press, 1983).

7. p. 95. D. L. Guemple, "Inuit socialization: A study of children as social actors in an Eskimo community." In I. Karigoudar, ed., *Childhood and Adolescence in Canada* (Toronto: McGraw-Hill Ryerson, 1979).

8. p. 95. R. Borofsky, *Making History: Pukapukan and Anthropological Constructions of Knowledge* (New York: Cambridge University Press, 1987).

9. p. 95. B. L. Hewlett and B. S. Hewlett, "Hunter-gatherer adolescence." In B. L. Hewlett, ed., *Adolescent Identity* (New York: Routledge, 2013).

10. p. 95. D. F. Lancy and M. A. Grove, "'Getting noticed': Middle childhood in cross-cultural perspective," *Human Nature*, **22**, 2011.

11. p. 95. D. F. Bjorkland, *Why Youth Is Not Wasted on the Young: Immaturity in Human Development* (New York: Blackwell, 2009). G. Principe, *Your Brain on Childhood: The Unexpected Side Effects of Classrooms, Ballparks, Family Rooms, and the Minivan* (New York: Prometheus, 2011).

The Roots of Schooling: Learning Must Be Paid For with Effort, Suffering, and Pain

1. p. 96. D. F. Lancy, "The social organization of learning: Initiation rituals and public schools," *Human Organization*, **34**, 1975.

2. p. 96. A. I. Richards, *Chisungu* (London: Faber and Faber, 1956).

3. p. 97. G. H. Herdt, "Sambia nose-bleeding rites and male proximity to women." In J. W. Stigler, R. A. Shweder, and G. H. Herdt, eds., *Cultural Psychology* (New York: Cambridge University Press, 1990).

4. p. 97. C. A. Markstrom, *Empowerment of North American Indian Girls: Ritual Expressions at Puberty* (Lincoln: University of Nebraska Press, 2008).

5. p. 97. W. Goldschmidt, *The Sebei: A Study in Adaptation* (New York: Holt, Rinehart and Winston, 1986).

6. p. 97. S.-J. Blakemore, "The social brain in adolescence," *Nature Reviews: Neuroscience*, **9**, 2008. There is a strong suggestion in the research on neurological changes during adolescence that the brain is shifting gears from task mastery to mastering the complexities of adult interpersonal relationships.

7. p. 97. H. B. Broch, *Growing Up Agreeably: Bonerate Childhood Observed* (Honolulu: University of Hawai'i Press, 1990).

8. p. 97. W. Murphy, "Secret knowledge as property and power in Kpelle society: Elders versus youth," *Africa*, **50**, 1980.

9. p. 97. D. Brooks, "Organization within disorder: The present and future of young people in the Ngaanyatjarra lands." In U. Eickelkamp, ed., *Growing up in Central Australia: New Anthropological Studies of Aboriginal Childhood and Adolescence* (Oxford: Berghahn Books, 2011).

10. p. 98. T. H. J. Marchand, *Minaret Building and Apprenticeship in Yemen* (Richmond: Curzon Press, 2001).

11. p. 98. J. A. Shelton, *As the Romans Did: A Sourcebook in Roman Social History* (Oxford: Oxford University Press, 1998).

12. p. 98. R. M. Dilley, "Secrets and skills: Apprenticeship among Tukolor weavers." In M. W. Coy, ed., *Apprenticeship: From Theory to Method and Back Again* (Albany: State University of New York Press, 1989).

13. p. 98. D. F. Lancy, "'First you must master pain:' The nature and purpose of apprenticeship," *Society for the Anthropology of Work Review*, **33**, 2012.

14. p. 98. J. Singleton, "Japanese folkcraft pottery apprenticeship: Cultural patterns of an educational institution." In M. W. Coy, ed., *Apprenticeship: From Theory to Method and Back Again* (Albany: State University of New York Press, 1989).

15. p. 98. F. Tanon, *A Cultural View on Planning: The Case of Weaving in Ivory Coast* (Tilburg: Tilburg University Press, 1994).

16. p. 99. N. Orme, *Medieval Schools: From Roman Britain to Renaissance England* (London: Yale University Press, 2006).
17. p. 99. H. W. F. Saggs, *Everyday Life in Babylonia and Assyria* (New York: Hippocrene Books, 1987).
18. p. 99. S. N. Kramer, *The Sumerians: Their History, Culture and Character* (Chicago: The University of Chicago Press, 1963).
19. p. 99. F. A. G. Beck, *Album of Greek Education: The Greeks at School and at Play* (Sydney: Cheiron Press, 1975).
20. p. 100. C. Laes, *Children in the Roman Empire* (Cambridge: Cambridge University Press, 2011).
21. p. 100. Orme, *Medieval Schools*.
22. p. 100. M. F. Durantini, *The Child in Seventeenth-Century Dutch Painting* (Ann Arbor, MI: UMI Research Press, 1983).
23. p. 100. Saggs, *Everyday Life in Babylonia and Assyria*.
24. p. 100. Orme, *Medieval Schools*.
25. p. 100. F. Gies and J. Gies, *Marriage and the Family in the Middle Ages* (New York: Harper and Row, 1987).

Coercive Pedagogy: When "Education" Means Compliance

1. p. 101. D. F. Lancy. *The Anthropology of Childhood: Cherubs, Chattel, Changelings*, 2nd edition (Cambridge: Cambridge University Press, 2015).
2. p. 102. J. Li, L. Wang, and K. Fischer, "The organization of Chinese shame concepts," *Cognition and Emotion*, **18**, 2004.
   P. Wu, L. Wang, and K. W. Fischer, "Similarities and differences in mothers' parenting of preschoolers in China and the United States," *International Journal of Behavioural Development*, **26**, 2002.
3. p. 102. P. J. Miller, T. L. Sandel, C.-H. Liang, and H. Fung, "Narrating transgressions in U.S. and Taiwan," *Ethos*, **29**, 2001.
4. p. 102. H. Geertz, *The Javanese Family: A Study of Kinship and Socialization* (New York: Free Press, 1961).
5. p. 102. C. Toren, *Making Sense of Hierarchy: Cognition as Social Process in Fiji* (Houndmills: Palgrave-Macmillan, 1990).
6. p. 102. T. R. Williams, *A Borneo Childhood: Enculturation in Dusun Society* (New York: Holt, Rinehart, and Winston, 1969).
7. p. 102. H. I. Hogbin, *A Guadalcanal Society: The Kaoka Speakers* (New York: Holt, Rinehart, and Winston, 1969).

8. p. 103. C. Collodi, *Pinocchio* (New York: Everyman's Library Children's Classics, Alfred A. Knopf, a division of Random House, 1883/2011).

9. p. 103. E. Ochs and C. Izquierdo, "Responsibility in childhood: Three developmental trajectories," *Ethos*, **37**, 2009.

10. p. 103. D. Freeman, *Margaret Mead and Samoa: The Making and Unmaking of an Anthropological Myth* (Cambridge, MA: Harvard University Press, 1983).

11. p. 103. M. J. Casimir, *Growing Up in a Pastoral Society: Socialization among Pashtu Nomads*, Kölner Ethnologische Beiträge (Cologne: Druck and Bindung, 2010).

12. p. 103. M. D. Ainsworth, *Infancy in Uganda: Infant Care and the Growth of Love* (Baltimore, MD: The Johns Hopkins University Press, 1967).

13. p. 104. W. Jankowiak, A. Joiner, and C. Khatib, "What observation studies can tell us about single child play patterns, gender, and changes in society," *Cross-Cultural Research*, **45**, 2011.

14. p. 105. B. L. Chapin, *Childhood in a Sri Lankan Village: Shaping Hierarchy and Desire* (New Brunswick, NJ: Rutgers University Press, 2014).

Of Course "Good" Teaching Is Rare—Why Should We Expect Otherwise?

1. p. 106. D. F. Bjorklund, *Why Youth Is Not Wasted on the Young* (Malden, MA: Blackwell, 2007).

2. p. 106. D. F. Lancy, *The Anthropology of Childhood: Cherubs, Chattel, Changelings*, 2nd edition (Cambridge: Cambridge University Press, 2015).
   See also M. Konner, "Is ADHD a disease of civilization?", PT blog post, September 13, 2010 at www.psychologytoday.com/blog/the-tangled-wing/201009/is-adhd-disease-civilization.

3. p. 106. S. D. Blum, *"I Love Learning; I Hate School": An Anthropology of College* (Ithaca, NY: Cornell University Press, 2016).

4. p. 107. P. R. Grendler, *Schooling in Renaissance Italy* (Baltimore, MD: The Johns Hopkins University Press, 1989).

5. pp. 107, 108. A. Howard, *Learning to Be Rotuman* (New York: Teachers College Press, 1970).

6. p. 108. D. F. Lancy and M. A. Grove, "The role of adults in children's learning." In D. F. Lancy, S. Gaskins, and J. Bock, eds., *The Anthropology of Learning in Childhood* (Lanham, MD: AltaMira Press, 2010).
7. p. 108. S. Goldman and A. Booker, "Making math a definition of the situation: Families as sites for mathematical practices," *Anthropology and Education Quarterly*, **40**, 2009.
8. pp. 108, 109. D. F. Lancy, K. Draper, and G. Boyce, "Parental influence on children's acquisition of reading," *Contemporary Issues in Reading*, **4**, 1989.
   p.109. C. Bergin, D. F. Lancy, and K. D. Draper, "Parents' interactions with beginning readers." In D. F. Lancy, ed., *Children's Emergent Literacy: From Research to Practice* (Westport, CT: Praeger, 1994).
9. p. 109. Bjorklund, *Why Youth Is Not Wasted on the Young.*
10. p. 109. M. Vandermaas-Peeler, J. Nelson, M. von der Heide, and E. Kelly, "Parental guidance with four-year-olds in literacy and play activities at home." In D. Kuschner, ed., *From Children to Red Hatters* (Lanham, MD: University Press of America).

Talking like a Book

1. p. 110. S. B. Heath, *Ways with Words* (Cambridge: Cambridge University Press, 1983).
2. p. 110. S. McNaughton, "Ways of parenting and cultural identity," *Culture and Psychology*, **2**, 1996.
3. p. 110. S. B. Heath, "What no bedtime story means: Narrative skills at home and school," *Language in Society*, **11**, 1982.
4. p. 110. C. E. Snow, W. S. Barnes, J. Chandler, and L. Hemphill, *Unfulfilled Expectations: Home and School Influences on Literacy* (Cambridge, MA: Harvard University Press, 1991).
5. p. 111. C. E. Snow and D. E. Beals, "Mealtime talk that supports literacy development," *New Directions for Child and Adolescent Development*, **111**, 2006.
6. p. 111. A. Sjögren-De Beauchaine, *The Bourgeoisie in the Dining Room: Meal Ritual and Cultural Process in Parisian Families of Today* (Stockholm: Institutet for Folkslivsforskining, 1998).

7. p. 111. M. Martini, "'What's new?' at the dinner table: Family dynamics during mealtimes in two cultural groups in Hawaii," *Early Development and Parenting*, 5, 1996.

8. p. 111. L. Sterponi and R. Santagata, "Mistakes in the classroom and at the dinner table: A comparison between socialization practices in Italy and the United States," *Crossroads of Language, Interaction and Culture*, 3, 2000.

9. p. 111. W. L. Haight and P. J. Miller, *Pretending at Home: Early Development in a Sociocultural Context* (Albany: State University of New York Press, 1993).

10. p. 111. M. Martini, "Features of home environments associated with children's school success," *Early Child Development and Care*, 111, 1995.

11. p. 111. D. F. Lancy, "The conditions that support emergent literacy." In D. F. Lancy, ed., *Children's Emergent Literacy: From Research to Practice* (Westport, CT: Praeger, 1994).

12. p. 111. D. E. Beals, "Eating and reading: Links between family conversations with preschoolers and later language and literacy." In D. K. Dickinson and P. O. Tabors, eds., *Beginning Literacy with Language* (Baltimore, MD: Paul H. Brooks, 2001).

13. p. 112. Lancy, "The conditions that support emergent literacy."

14. p. 112. G. L. Doctoroff, J. A. Greer, and D. H. Arnold, "The relationship between social behavior and emergent literacy among preschool boys and girls," *Journal of Applied Developmental Psychology*, 27, 2006.

15. p. 113. E. N. Goody, "Dynamics of the emergence of sociocultural institutional practices." In D. R. Olson and M. Cole, eds., *Technology, Literacy, and the Evolution of Society* (Mahwah, NJ: Erlbaum, 2006).

16. p. 113. S. L. Macedo, "Indigenous school policies and politics: The sociopolitical relationship of Wayãpi Amerindians to Brazilian and French Guyana schooling," *Anthropology and Education Quarterly*, 40, 2009.

17. p. 113. Lancy, "The conditions that support emergent literacy."

18. p. 113. M. de Haan, "Inter-subjectivity in models of learning and teaching: Reflection from a study of teaching and learning in a Mexican Mazhua Community." In S. Chaiklin, ed., *The Theory and Practice of Cultural-Historical Psychology* (Aarhus: Aarhus University Press, 2001).

19. p. 113. ACT: The Condition of College and Career Readiness—2014 (Iowa City: American College Testing Service, 2014), available at www.act.org/content/act/en/research/condition-of-college-and-career-readiness-report-2014.html?page=0&chapter=0.

p.113. Anonymous, *To Read or Not to Read: A Question of National Consequence* (Washington, DC: National Endowment for the Arts, November 2014), available at www.arts.gov/sites/default/files/ToRead.pdf.

20. p. 113. R. C. Anderson, E. H. Hiebert, J. A. Scott, and I. A. G. Wilkinson, *Becoming a Nation of Readers: Report of the Commission on Reading* (Washington, DC: National Academy of Education, 1985).

Chapter 7: The Consequences of Raising "Unique Individuals"

1. p. 115. H. I. Hogbin, *A Guadalcanal Society: The Kaoka Speakers* (New York: Holt, Rinehart, and Winston, 1969).
2. p. 116. https://en.wikipedia.org/wiki/Zootopia.
3. p. 116. H. Keller, J. Borke, B. Lamm, A. Lohaus, and R. Dz. Yovsi, "Developing patterns of parenting in two cultural communities," *International Journal of Behavioral Development*, **35**, 2010.
4. p. 117. A. Paugh and C. Izquierdo, "Why is this a battle every night? Negotiating food and eating in American dinnertime interaction," *Journal of Linguistic Anthropology*, **19**, 2009.
5. p. 117. C. C. Delistraty, "The importance of eating together," *The Atlantic*, July 18, 2014.
6. p. 118. T. Kremer-Sadlik and K. Gutiérrez, "Homework and recreation." In E. Ochs and T. Kremer-Sadlik, eds., *Fast-Forward Families: Home, Work, and Relationships* (Berkeley: University of California Press, 2013).
7. p. 119. E. Ochs and M. Beck, "Dinner." In E. Ochs, and T. Kremer-Sadlik, eds., *Fast-Forward Families: Home, Work, and Relationships* (Berkeley: University of California Press, 2013).
8. p. 119. Delistraty, "The importance of eating together."
9. p. 119. E. Ochs, C. Taylor, D. Rudolph, and R. Smith, "Storytelling as a theory-building activity," *Discourse Processes*, **15**, 1992.

M. Martini, "Features of home environments associated with children's school success," *Early Child Development and Care*, **111**, 1995.

D. E. Beals, "Eating and reading: Links between family conversations with preschoolers and later language and literacy." In D. K. Dickinson and P. O. Tabors, eds., *Beginning Literacy with Language* (Baltimore, MD: Paul H. Brooks, 2001).

10. p. 120. M. Martini, "'What's new?' at the dinner table: Family dynamics during mealtimes in two cultural groups in Hawaii," *Early Development and Parenting*, 5, 1996.

11. p. 120. J. Schor, *Born to Buy: The Commercialized Child and the New Consumer Culture* (New York: Simon & Schuster, 2005).

What's in a Name?

1. p. 121. D. F. Lancy, *The Anthropology of Childhood: Cherubs, Chattel, Changelings*, 2nd edition (Cambridge: Cambridge University Press, 2015).

2. p. 122. P. E. Bugos Jr. and L. M. McCarthy, "Ayoreo infanticide: A case study." In G. Hausfater and S. B. Hrdy, eds., *Infanticide: Comparative and Evolutionary Perspectives* (New York: Aldine, 1984).

3. p. 122. K. Takeuchi, "Food restriction and social identity of Aka forager adolescents in the Republic of Congo." In B. L. Hewlett, ed., *Adolescent Identity: Evolutionary, Cultural and Developmental Perspectives* (New York: Routledge, 2013).

4. p. 122. B. Rawson, "Adult–child relationships in Roman society." In B. Rawson, ed., *Marriage, Divorce, and Children in Ancient Rome* (Canberra: Clarendon Press, 1991).

5. p. 122. A. Gottlieb, "Luring your child into this life: A Beng path for infant care." In J. DeLoache and A. Gottlieb, eds., *A World of Babies* (Cambridge: Cambridge University Press, 2000).

6. p. 122. J. W. Sprott, *Raising Young Children in an Alaskan Iñupiaq Village: The Family, Cultural, and Village Environment of Rearing* (Westport, CT: Bergin and Garvey, 2002).

7. p. 122. M. Zeitlin, "My child is my crown: Yoruba parental theories and practices in early childhood." In S. Harkness and C. M. Super, eds., *Parents' Cultural Belief Systems: Their Origins, Expressions, and Consequences* (New York: Guilford Press, 1996).

8. p. 123. R. Stasch, *Society of Others: Kinship and Mourning in a West Papuan Place* (Berkeley: University of California Press, 2009).

9. p. 123. W. Irons, "Why do the Yomut raise more sons than daughters?" In L. Cronk, N. Chagnon, and W. Irons, eds., *Adaptation and Human Behavior: An Anthropological Perspective* (New York: Aldine, 2000).

10. p. 124. P. Riesman, *First Find Your Child a Good Mother* (New Brunswick, NJ: Rutgers University Press, 1992).

11. p. 124. L. Batels, "Birth customs and birth songs of the Macha Galla," *Ethnology*, **8**, 1969.

12. p. 124. Anonymous, "Swedish parents keep two-year-old's gender secret," *The Local: Sweden's News in English*, June 23, 2009, available at www.theguardian.com/lifeandstyle/2010/jun/22/swedish-parents-baby-gender.

13. p. 124. J. Contrera, "Their Tube: When every moment of childhood can be recorded and shared, what happens to childhood?", *Washington Post: The Screen Age*, Dec. 7, 2016, available at www.washingtonpost.com/sf/style/2016/12/07/when-every-moment-of-childhood-can-be-recorded-and-shared-what-happens-to-childhood.

14. pp. 124, 125. C. Gross-Loh, *Parenting without Borders* (New York: Avery, 2013).

15. p. 125. L. Heffernan, "Our push for 'passion,' and why it harms kids," *New York Times*, April 8, 2015, available at parenting.blogs.nytimes.com/2015/04/08/our-push-for-passion-and-why-it-harms-kids/?emc=eta1&_r=0.

16. p. 125. Y. A. Joyce, "Are you raising nice kids? A Harvard psychologist gives 5 ways to raise them to be kind," *Washington Post*, July 18, 2014.

17. p. 126. J. Henrich, S. J. Heine, and A. Norenzayan, "The weirdest people in the world?", *Behavioural and Brain Sciences*, **33**, 2010.

18. p. 127. M. Konnikova, "Why your name matters," *New Yorker*, December 19, 2013, available at www.newyorker.com/tech/elements/why-your-name-matters.

19. p. 127. http://inch.stormpages.com.

Trash Talking or Taking Out the Trash

1. pp. 127, 128. W. Klein, A. Graesch, and C. Izquierdo, "Children and chores: A mixed-methods study of children's household work in Los Angeles families," *Anthropology of Work Review*, **30**, 2009.

2. p. 128. E. Ochs and C. Izquierdo, "Responsibility in childhood: Three developmental trajectories," *Ethos*, **37**, 2009.

3. p. 128, 129, 130, 131. D. F. Lancy, *The Anthropology of Childhood: Cherubs, Chattel, Changelings*, 2nd edition (Cambridge: Cambridge University Press, 2015).

4. pp. 129, 130. I. Golovnev, *Malenkaya Katerina* (Tiny Katerina), documentary film (Ekaterinburg: Ethnographic Bureau Studio, 2004).

5. p. 131. D. F. Lancy, "The chore curriculum." In G. Spittler and M. Bourdillion, eds., *African Children at Work: Working and Learning in Growing Up* (Berlin: LIT Verlag, 2012).

6. p. 131. M. H. MacElroy, *Work and Play in Colonial Days* (New York: Macmillan, 1917).

7. p. 132. V. A. Zelizer, *Pricing the Priceless Child: The Changing Social Value of Children* (New York: Basic Books, 1985).

8. p. 132. A. S. Kusserow, *American Individualisms: Child Rearing and Social Class in Three Neighborhoods* (New York: Palgrave Macmillan, 2004).

9. p. 133. H. Rheingold, "Little children's participation in the work of adults, a nascent prosocial behavior," *Child Development*, **53**, 1982. In this same report, the author also noted, "In informal questioning before the study began, the parents uniformly reported at least one task in which the children participated at home. Rather than expressing satisfaction in the children's efforts, many parents reported that to avoid what they viewed as interference they tried to accomplish the chores while the children were taking their naps" (p. 122).

10. p. 133. F. Warneken and M. Tomasello, "Altruistic helping in human infants and young chimpanzees," *Science*, **311**(5765), 2006. F. Warneken and M. Tomasello, "The roots of human altruism," *British Journal of Psychology*, **100**, 2009.

11. p. 133. T. El-Rahi, "Childhood chores are a predictor of success: The sooner the kids start, the better," *Intellectual Takeout*, January 22, 2016, available at www.intellectualtakeout.org/blog/childhood-chores-are-predictor-success.

12. p. 133. A. Stuart, "Age appropriate chores for children: Chore ideas and allowances," WebMD, 2013, at www.webmd.com/parenting/features/chores-for-children.

Failure to Launch

1. p. 134. http://www.paramount.com/movies/failure-launch. Of course, not all the twenty-somethings living at home have abandoned their launch like Tripp. A significant number are living at home to save money, and thereby lighten their debt as they prepare to launch.

2. p. 135. M. A. Grove and D. F. Lancy, "Cultural views of life phases." In J. D. Wright, ed., *International Encyclopedia of Social and Behavioral Sciences*, 2nd edition (Oxford: Elsevier, 2015).

3. p. 135. B. Rogoff, "Learning by observing and pitching in to family and community endeavors: An orientation," *Human Development*, **57**, 2014.

4. p. 135. R. W. White, "Motivation reconsidered: The concept of competence," *Psychological Review*, **66**, 1959.

5. p. 135. F. de Waal, *The Ape and the Sushi Master* (New York: Basic Books, 2001).

6. pp. 135, 136. H. Rheingold, "Little children's participation in the work of adults, a nascent prosocial behavior," *Child Development*, **53**, 1982.

7. p. 136. L. Alcalá, B. Rogoff, R. Mejía-Arauz, A. D. Coppens, and A. L. Dexter, "Children's initiative in contributions to family work in indigenous-heritage and cosmopolitan communities in Mexico," *Human Development*, **57**, 2014.

8. pp. 136, 137. A. S. Kusserow, *American Individualisms: Child Rearing and Social Class in Three Neighborhoods* (New York: Palgrave Macmillan, 2004).

9. p. 137. C. Sinha, "Situated selves: Learning to be a learner." In J. Bliss, R. Säljö, and P. Light, eds., *Learning Sites: Social and Technological Resources for Learning* (Oxford: Pergamon, 1999).

10. pp. 137, 138. D. F. Lancy and M. A. Grove, "'Getting noticed': Middle childhood in cross-cultural perspective," *Human Nature*, **22**, 2011.

11. p. 139. R. Willerslev, *Soul Hunters: Hunting, Animism, and Personhood among the Siberian Yukaghirs* (Berkeley: University of California Press, 2007).

12. p. 139. M. Mitterauer and R. Sieder, *The European Family: Patriarchy to Partnership from the Middle Ages to the Present* (Chicago: The University of Chicago Press, 1997).

13. p. 140. S. C. Leavitt, "The *bikhet* mystique: Masculine identity and patterns of rebellion among Bumbita adolescent males."

In G. H. Herdt and S. Leavitt, eds., *Adolescence in Pacific Island Societies* (Pittsburgh, PA: University of Pittsburgh Press, 1998).

14. p. 141. A. Ascher, "Failure to launch syndrome," *Huffington Post*, May 2, 2015.

    H. Schiffrin, M. Liss, and H. Miles-McLean, "Helping or hovering? The effects of helicopter parenting on college students' well-being," *Journal of Child and Family Studies*, **23**, 2014.

15. pp. 141, 142. L. Sax, *Boys Adrift: The Five Factors Driving the Growing Epidemic of Unmotivated Boys and Underachieving Young Men* (New York: Basic, 2007).

Chapter 8: Summary and Speculation

Gazing into the Crystal Ball

1. p. 158. B. Sandlin, "Children and the Swedish Welfare State: From different to familiar." In P. S. Fass and G. Michael, eds., *Reinventing Childhood after World War II* (Philadelphia: University of Pennsylvania Press, 2012).

2. p. 159. M. Yousafzai and C. Lamb, *I Am Malala: The Girl Who Stood Up for Education and Was Shot by the Taliban* (Boston, MA: Little, Brown & Co., 2013).

3. p. 159. R. A. LeVine, S. LeVine, B. Schnell-Anzola, M. L. Rowe, and E. Dexter, *Literacy and Mothering: How Women's Schooling Changes the Lives of the World's Children* (New York: Oxford University Press, 2012).

4. p. 161. M. V. Flinn and B. G. England, "Childhood stress and family environment," *Current Anthropology*, **36**, 1995.

5. p. 161. T. Walker, "The joyful, illiterate kindergartners of Finland," *The Atlantic*, October 1, 2015, available at www.theatlantic.com/ education/archive/2015/10/the-joyful-illiterate-kindergartners-of-finland/408325.

6. p. 161. O. Goldhill, "Psychologists recommend children be bored in the summer," *Quartz: The Art of Parenting*, June 16, 2016, available at qz.com/704723/to-be-more-self-reliant-children-need-boring-summers.

7. p. 162. A. Duckworth, *Grit: The Power of Passion and Perseverance* (New York: Scribner, 2016).

D. Denby, "The limits of 'grit'," *New Yorker*, June 21, 2016, available at www.newyorker.com/culture/culture-desk/the-limits-of-grit?mbid=nl_160621_Daily&CNDID=23488343&spMailingID=9091390&spUserID=MTE3MTcxOTAyMzE5S0&spJobID=942069823&spReportId=OTQyMDY5ODIzS0.

8. p. 162. A. Rathi and J. Anderson, "The science of getting your kids to eat more vegetables," *Quartz: The Art of Parenting*, June 25, 2016, available at http://qz.com/701128/the-science-behind-getting-your-kids-to-eat-everything.

9. p. 163. M. Teague, "Incidents of toddlers shooting others or themselves increasing, data shows," *The Guardian*, May 2, 2016, available at www.theguardian.com/us-news/2016/may/02/toddler-shooting-gun-control-children?CMP=share_btn_fb.

Chapter 9: The Backstory

1. p. 164. D. F. Lancy, "Accounting for variability in mother–child play," *American Anthropologist*, **109**(2), 2007.

2. p. 164. C. Shea, "Leave the kids alone," *Boston Globe*, July 15, 2007, available at www.boston.com/news/globe/ideas/articles/2007/07/15/leave_those_kids_alone.

3. p. 165. http://bnp.binghamton.edu/projects/past-projects/empowering-neighborhoods-and-restoring-outdoor-play.

4. p. 166. D. F. Lancy, *The Anthropology of Childhood: Cherubs, Chattel, Changelings*, 2nd edition (Cambridge: Cambridge University Press, 2015).

5. p. 166. www.nytimes.com/2015/02/01/opinion/sunday/the-only-baby-book-youll-ever-need.html?_r=0.

6. p. 168. D. F. Lancy, *Playing on the Mother-Ground: Cultural Routines for Children's Development* (New York: Guilford, 1996).

Index